The Carefree-Ease Record

W0113983

Other Books by David Hinton

WRITING

Orient
Wild Earth, Wild Mind
China Root
Awakened Cosmos
Desert
The Wilds of Poetry
Existence: A Story
Hunger Mountain
Fossil Sky

TRANSLATION

The Blue-Cliff Record
The Way of Ch'an: Essential Texts of the Original Tradition
The Selected Poems of Tu Fu: Expanded and Newly Translated
No-Gate Gateway
I Ching: The Book of Change
The Late Poems of Wang An-shih
The Four Chinese Classics
Classical Chinese Poetry: An Anthology
The Selected Poems of Wang Wei
The Mountain Poems of Meng Hao-jan
Mountain Home: The Wilderness Poetry of Ancient China
The Mountain Poems of Hsieh Ling-yün
Tao Te Ching
The Selected Poems of Po Chü-i
The Analects
Mencius
Chuang Tzu: The Inner Chapters
The Late Poems of Meng Chiao
The Selected Poems of Li Po
The Selected Poems of T'ao Ch'ien
The Selected Poems of Tu Fu

THE
CAREFREE-EASE
RECORD

TRANSLATED BY

David Hinton

SHAMBHALA

SHAMBHALA PUBLICATIONS, INC.
2129 13th Street
Boulder, Colorado 80302
www.shambhala.com

Cover art: The Joy of Fish *by Chou Tung-ch'ing. The Metropolitan Museum of Art,
New York. From the Collection of A. W. Bahr, Purchase, Fletcher Fund, 1947.*
Interior design: Steve Dyer

9 8 7 6 5 4 3 2 1

FIRST EDITION
Printed in the United States of America

Shambhala Publications makes every effort to print on acid-free, recycled paper.
Shambhala Publications is distributed worldwide by Penguin Random House, Inc.,
and its subsidiaries.

LIBRARY OF CONGRESS CATALOGING-IN-PUBLICATION DATA
Names: Zhengjue, 1091–1157, author. | Hinton, David, 1954– translator. |
Xingxiu, 1166–1246. Ts'ung jung lu.
Title: The carefree-ease record / translated by David Hinton.
Description: First edition. | Boulder, Colorado: Shambhala, [2025] | Translation of texts
attributed to Zhengjue from the Ts'ung jung lu. | Includes bibliographical references and
index. | Text in English. Translation from Chinese.
Identifiers: LCCN 2024044810 | ISBN 9781645472711 (trade paperback)
Subjects: LCSH: Enlightenment (Zen Buddhism)—Early works to 1800. |
Meditation—Buddhism—Early works to 1800.
Classification: LCC BQ9288 .Z481213 2025 | DDC 294.3/443—dc23/eng/20250123
LC record available at https://lccn.loc.gov/2024044810

Contents

Introduction   ix

The Carefree-Ease Record   1

1. World-Honored-One Ascended   2
2. Bodhidharma Vast Expanse Absence   4
3. East Indian Invites Patriarch   6
4. World-Honored-One Pointed   8
5. Source Clearwater Rice Price   10
6. Way-Entire Bright Dark   12
7. Medicine Ascended and Sat   14
8. Hundred-Elder Wild Fox   16
9. Wellspring-South Chopped Kitten   18
10. Five-Terrace Shop-Woman   20
11. Cloud-Gate Two Sickness   22
12. Earth-Hoard Planting Fields   24
13. Dark-Enigma Blind Donkey   26
14. Attendant Expanse Offered Tea   28
15. Reliance Mountain Planted Shovel   30
16. Flax-Canyon Sangha-Staff   32
17. Dharma-Eye Hair-Width   34
18. Visitation-Land Dog Nature   36
19. Cloud-Gate Sumeru Mountain   38
20. Earth-Hoard Cutting Clean   40
21. Cloud-Crag Sweeping Path   42
22. Crag-Summit KHO-AAA!   44
23. Yokel-Patriarch Faced Wall   46
24. Snow-Peak Look Viper   48

25. Salt-Legal Rhinoxeros Fan   50
26. Reliance Mountain Pointed Snow   52
27. Dharma-Eye Pointed Blinds   54
28. Shelter-Nation Three Humilities   56
29. Wind-Source Iron Ox   58
30. Tumble-Vast Kalpa-Fires   60
31. Cloud-Gate Dew Pillars   62
32. Reliance Mountain Mind Circumstance   64
33. Three-Sage Golden Fish   66
34. Wind-Source Dust Mote   68
35. Far-Waters Knelt Bowed   70
36. Way-Entire Was Unwell   72
37. River-Act Karma Curse   74
38. Dark-Enigma Thusness-Clarity   76
39. Visitation-Land Wash Bowl   78
40. Cloud-Gate Bright Dark   80
41. Far-Waters Facing Death   82
42. Prajna-Devotion Water-Jar   84
43. Gauze Mountain Appearing Disappearing   86
44. Solar-Burgeon Wondrous Wings   88
45. Enlightenment Sutra Four Practices   90
46. Lumen-Whole Done Practicing   92
47. Visitation-Land Cypress Tree   94
48. Vimalakirti Dharma-Gate Nonduality   96
49. Fathom Mountain Altar Offerings   98
50. Snow-Peak What's This   100
51. Dharma-Eye Boat Land   102
52. Twofold Mountain Dharma Body   104
53. Yellow-Bitterroot Nibbling Dregs   106
54. Cloud-Gate Great Compassion   108
55. Snow-Peak Head-Cook   110
56. Spirit-Lightning White Rabbit   112
57. Solar-Strict One Thing   114
58. Diamond Sutra Worthless Bonehead   116
59. Azure-Forest Dead Snake   118
60. Iron-Grinder Water-Buffalo   120
61. Heaven-Peak Single Path   122

CONTENTS

62. Mongrol-Grain Awakening Vanished   124
63. Visitation-Land Asked Death   126
64. Adept-Beckon Transmission Continues   128
65. First Mountain Young Bride   130
66. Nine-Peak Beginning End   132
67. Garland Sutra *Prajna*-Wisdom   134
68. Stealth Mountain Swings Sword   136
69. Wellspring-South Water-Buffalo   138
70. Tribute Asked Original-Nature   140
71. Kingfisher-Cliff Mountain Eyelids   142
72. Bull's-Eye Altar Monkey   144
73. Twofold Mountain Done Honoring   146
74. Dharma-Eye Natureless Nameless   148
75. Perennial Inner-Pattern Talisman   150
76. First Mountain Three Times   152
77. Reliance Mountain Well Enough   154
78. Cloud-Gate Gruel-Cake   156
79. Perpetua-Sands Step Beyond   158
80. Dragon-Fang Passed Clapper   160
81. Dark-Enigma-Sands Traveled   162
82. Cloud-Gate Sound Color   164
83. Way-I Visiting Doctor   166
84. Million-Million One Finger   168
85. Prajna-Devotion Shrine Tower   170
86. Dark-Enigma Great Awakening   172
87. Scatter Mountain Presence Absence   174
88. *Hewn-Beam* Not Seeing   176
89. Fathom Mountain No Grass   178
90. Reliance Mountain Sounds Mallet   180
91. Wellspring-South Peony Blooming   182
92. Cloud-Gate Perfect Jewel   184
93. Yokel-Patriarch Not Understanding   186
94. Fathom Mountain Was Unwell   188
95. Dark-Enigma Draws Horizon   190
96. Nine-Peak Didn't Approve   192
97. Radiant-Alike Regal Hat   194
98. Fathom Mountain Cutting Clean   196

99. Cloud-Gate Bowl Pail   198
100. Jewel-Fang Rivers Mountains   200

Notes   203
Key Terms: An Outline of Ch'an's Conceptual World   215
Glossary of Buddhist Terms   231
Index to Ch'an Teachers
  1. English Names with Chinese Equivalents   235
  2. Chinese Names with English Equivalents   238
Sangha-Cases Included in Other Collections   241

Introduction

WHAT IS THIS STRANGE and wondrous book all about? The title says it all: *Carefree-Ease* (從容), a term borrowed across fifteen centuries from Chuang Tzu, seminal Taoist sage from the fourth century B.C.E. Chuang Tzu famously uses the term to describe fish joyfully drifting here and there in a river—the scene rendered exquisitely in the painting on this book's cover, Chou Tung-ch'ing's *The Joy of Fish*. For Chuang Tzu, *carefree-ease* describes the joy of moving integral to earth and Cosmos as they unfurl effortlessly through their perennial transformations. It's an enlightened state that animals like those fish inhabit naturally and that humans rarely master. But if you do, says *The Carefree-Ease Record* (Case 35), it is profound realization:

> Live like a red-fin adrift full of contentment, rippling in the current,
> then you fathom it all and depend on nothing: transformed, liberated
>
> you wander this realm alone, enlightenment seen all the way through,
> wander at ease in the wild joy and delight infusing all beneath heaven.

Chuang Tzu says elsewhere that a sage who moves with this *carefree-ease* is "like a dragon, like a tiger," and like "a dragon seething in the stillness of death, thunder booming in the dark abyss of silence." This begins to reveal the philosophical depth of *carefree-ease*. For the tiger exemplifies dynamic spontaneity and fierce directness, and would eventually become an image for the Ch'an master. And dragon: dragon pervades ancient Chinese culture, where it was feared and revered as the awesome force of change, as the embodiment of all creation and all destruction. To move through life with *carefree-ease* is, then, to take on the elemental nature of tiger and dragon.

This *carefree-ease*, in a host of different formulations, echoes through the Ch'an tradition as a principal dimension of enlightenment, culminating here in *The Carefree-Ease Record*. Indeed, it was such a fixture in Ch'an thought that, a few decades after *The Carefree-Ease Record* appeared, we find the great poet Yang Wan-li playfully undermining this idea (in the Ch'an tradition of dismantling all certainties of idea and teaching):

Report from Chuang Tzu's River

Ten miles of emerald ripples and *carefree-ease* fish, this river
keeps leaving, seething swells of this human realm, no return.

A shoreline egret has already eaten its fill. Nothing left to do,
it stands there in morning light, fussing over its snowy robes.

But to understand *carefree-ease* in all its philosophical depth, as well as Ch'an and *The Carefree-Ease Record* more generally, we must understand Ch'an's full conceptual framework. We speak now of Ch'an (or using the later Japanese pronunciation, Zen) Buddhism, but the original Ch'an tradition does not use that term. It speaks only of Ch'an: the Ch'an house/school (禪家), Ch'an ancestral tradition (禪宗), Ch'an gate (禪門). And indeed, Ch'an is resolutely anti-Buddhist. Indeed, *The Carefree-Ease Record* begins in chapter 1 with Ch'an's anti-Buddhist clarity brilliantly dismantling the vast mythological realms of conventional Buddhism and any reverence for the teachings even of Buddha himself. And that dismantling continues throughout every philosophical dimension of the book.

Rather than a school of Buddhism, Ch'an is a Buddhist-inflected form of Taoism, China's native system of spiritual philosophy. Buddhism's largest contribution may have been its model of an institutional setting for practice—but core Ch'an, true to its Taoist roots, never stopped undermining that very institution. And here, that anti-Buddhist spirit is reflected already in the book's title, deriving as it does from Taoist sources. In their titles, previous translations have translated 從容 (*Carefree-Ease*) as *Serenity* or *Equanimity*. This is yet another instance of how the assumption that Ch'an is a form of conventional Buddhism infects modern translation and understanding of Ch'an texts—and so, how they are mistakenly perceived in contemporary Zen. Although Chuang

Tzu's *carefree-ease* does involve dimensions of profound tranquility, the term has nothing to do with the "serenity" or "equanimity" of Buddhism's aspiration for nirvana-peace.

Ch'an's philosophical framework emerged over two millennia prior to the *Carefree-Ease Record*'s appearance, originating in the seminal Taoist texts: *I Ching*, *Tao Te Ching*, and *Chuang Tzu*. Taoist thought is best described as a spiritual ecology, the central concept of which is Tao, or Way. *Tao* originally meant "way," as in pathway or roadway, a meaning it has kept. But Lao Tzu and Chuang Tzu, the originary Taoist thinkers, redefined it as a generative cosmological process, an ontological path-*Way* by which things come into existence, evolve through their lives, and then go out of existence, only to be transformed and reemerge in a new form. To understand Tao, we must approach it at its deepest ontological and cosmological levels, where it might be described as an "existence-tissue" that can be divided provisionally into two aspects: Absence (無) and Presence (有), concepts that represent the fundamental substrate of Ch'an practice.

Presence is simply the empirical universe, which the ancients described as the ten thousand things in constant transformation; and *Absence* is the generative tissue from which this ever-changing realm of Presence perpetually emerges. Or more properly, Absence is the existence-tissue seen not as ten thousand distinct forms, but as a single undifferentiated tissue that is boundlessly generative—the source of those ten thousand individual things. Way can be understood as the generative process through which all things arise and pass away as Absence burgeons forth into the great transformation of Presence. This is simply an ontological description of natural process, and it is perhaps most immediately manifest in the seasonal cycle: the pregnant emptiness of Absence in winter, Presence's burgeoning forth in spring, the fullness of its flourishing in summer, and its dying back into Absence in autumn.

Dwelling as integral to Tao at the deepest level is Ch'an's primary concern, and as we will see, the wilderness cosmology of Absence and Presence is central to Ch'an practice. Another appellation for the Ch'an school was 宗門, meaning most simply "ancestral gate" or "gate of the ancestors," hence a school of thought or practice handed down from the ancestors, wherein "gate" suggests both "an entranceway to a household" (as in traditional Chinese dwellings) and "an entranceway to insight."

But more fundamentally, 宗門 means "source-ancestral gate," suggesting Ch'an is the gate into the source-ancestral. This source-ancestral is nothing other than Absence (無: *wu*), the ancestral ontological/cosmological source. And inhabiting this source-ancestral as home-ground is indeed the essence of Ch'an.

Taoist ontology/cosmology was taken for granted in ancient China by both Ch'an practitioners and all artist-intellectuals. These concepts appear, therefore, in texts like the *Carefree-Ease Record* without explanation. The Key Terms appendix at the end of this book (p. 215) defines those foundational concepts, and can be read straight through as a fuller description of Ch'an's conceptual world. That conceptual world is described more completely in my *China Root: Taoism, Ch'an, and Original Zen*. And the development of that framework through the millennia of proto-Ch'an and Ch'an texts in China is traced in my *The Way of Ch'an: Essential Texts from the Original Tradition*.

The Ch'an written tradition cultivated Taoism's source-ancestral dwelling over the centuries, primarily in prose works by and about Ch'an masters, records of their lives and teachings. These records contain a great deal of conventional explanatory teaching, which is necessary to prepare students for Ch'an's wordless insight, its boundless depths. That direct insight is conveyed in the more literary dimension of those records: poetry, which is perfectly suited to the quick, deep insights of Ch'an, and storytelling typified by poetic distillation: enigmatic sayings and wild antics intended to upend reason and tease mind past the limitations of logical thought. These are performative, rather than explanatory—enacting insight, rather than talking about it. As such, they operate with poetic wildness and immediacy, instead of the usual discursive explanation. They thereby come as close as language can to those depths of Ch'an insight that lie outside words and teaching.

About five centuries after Ch'an's beginnings in the fourth and fifth centuries c.e., teachers began drawing especially revealing moments from the records of earlier teachers, moments that distill the essential insights of Ch'an, and using them as teaching tools. These scraps of story came to be known as *kung-an* (公案, now widely known in its Japanese pronunciation: *koan*). *Kung-an* means a "law-court case," or more literally a "public case," and it was adopted to the Ch'an situation for a number of reasons. First, a *kung-an* presents a factual situation that needs to be understood accurately, like a court case—understood, however, at a level that precedes thought and analysis. Second, each *kung-an* represents a kind of precedent to which practitioners can refer. And finally, masters originally conducted *kung-an* training in "public," when the entire monastic community was gathered together. Hence the translation adopted here: "sangha-case" (*sangha* meaning "a Buddhist community").

Eventually, in tenth-century Sung Dynasty China, teachers began gathering these sangha-cases into collections used for training students. Three of these collections established themselves as the enduring classics, perennially employed over the centuries in China, then Japan, and on into Zen practice around the world today: *The Blue-Cliff Record* (ca. 1040 C.E.), *The Carefree-Ease Record* (ca. 1145), and *No-Gate Gateway* (1228). Such sangha-case collections are now generally treated by most teachers as mere collections of stories that provide an occasion for teaching. They are instead masterpieces of classical Chinese literature, each with its own particular way into the essence of Ch'an insight: *The Blue-Cliff Record* dismantles authority and meaning to open us into the wordless awakening we already possess; *No-Gate Gateway* explores the depths of Absence; and as we have begun to see, *The Carefree-Ease Record* reveals *carefree-ease* as perhaps the essence of enlightened liberation. And whatever their particular approach, they are all carefully constructed literary/philosophical texts designed to create—in and of themselves and without further explanation—a direct and immediate literary experience in the reader: the experience of awakening's wordless depths. In this, they are the culmination of Ch'an literary creation—a new and unique and profound literary form that combines poetry and zany micro-tales to explore the deepest nature of mind and reality with insight and humor.

This is typical of the Chinese philosophical tradition, where the seminal classics are all literary in nature—poetry and storytelling replete with interesting characters engaged in revealing conversation and events. For philosophy in ancient China was all about immediate experiential wisdom, rather than the abstract truths that occupy the Western tradition. And so, the world we enter in Ch'an literature is a community not of religious acolytes, but of philosophers exploring the deep nature of things together, and in a way that is experientially transforming. Within this literary world, a sangha-case contains virtually no explanation, and therefore represents the most fully realized vehicle of Ch'an's "separate transmission outside all teaching." Sangha-cases are the culmination of Ch'an's historical development, because they incorporate and assume all of the insights and strategies that Ch'an had developed over the centuries. And once those insights and strategies are familiar, the seeming paradox of sangha-cases becomes approachable.

Echoing *The Blue-Cliff Record*, *The Carefree-Ease Record* (從容錄) is constructed of one hundred chapters, each containing a sangha-case and a "commentary" in the form of a *gatha* (sutra-poem). This form extends a tradition wherein classic texts included commentary that was considered an integral part of the text and a major philosophical genre in its own right, a tradition stretching all the way back to the beginning: the *I Ching*, China's first book, is virtually all "commentary."

In *The Carefree-Ease Record*, this structure divides neatly into two levels written by two different Ch'an masters: a primary text and a secondary text. The primary text was written around 1145 C.E. by the illustrious Wisdom-Expanse (Hung-Chih: 1091–1157), a very prominent teacher who produced an especially large body of writing. This primary text includes two elements: first, the sangha-cases themselves, scraps of story that Wisdom-Expanse selected from the Ch'an tradition and retold with revisions that suited his literary purposes, most often insightful distillation that highlights each story's essence; and second, the *gathas*, poetic "commentaries" that provide additional layers of insight no less important as direct teaching than the sangha-cases themselves. Not commentary in any normal sense, these *gathas* are at most only tangentially related to the sangha-cases, veering instead in their own directions, exploring their own new insights. Those insights inevitably further Ch'an's focus on defying the kinds of easy answers commentary traditionally gives. So, the *gathas* are concise and insightful and challenging in much the same way as the sangha-cases themselves. They represent a continuation of the direct insight enacted by the sangha-cases, teaching as direct and close to the immediate experience of wordless insight as we can get in language. And it must be said, they often display remarkable poetic power, with a flair for flights into quasi-surreal spaces, dramatic gestures, and descriptions of wild *carefree-ease* freedom.

The secondary text came eighty years later, when a Ch'an master named Ten-Thousand Pines (Wan Sung: 1166–1246) added an extensive commentary to Wisdom-Expanse's text. Although there is some direct teaching here, this is commentary in a more conventional sense, operating primarily as secondary explication. The compilation of these two texts became *The Carefree-Ease Record.*

Here we encounter the conflict between Ch'an as direct mind-to-mind transmission outside of words and explanations (primary text) and the natural belief that understanding comes through explanatory teaching (secondary text). This conflict between direct wordless transmission and explanatory teaching is a problematic running all through the Ch'an tradition. Explanation is certainly necessary as preparation for that direct insight, and it serves institutional Ch'an's need for teaching programs, etc. But in the end, it precludes wordless awakening. It was therefore reviled by Ch'an teachers, who also resisted institutional structures of all kinds (even while generally operating within them). Keeping faith with Ch'an as direct transmission, this translation presents only Wisdom-Expanse's sangha-cases and their companion *gathas*, the direct teaching. Hopefully the explanations here in this Introduction and in the Key Terms appendix (and beyond in *China Root* and *The Way of Ch'an*) are sufficient preparation for that direct teaching.

Indeed, in other writings Wisdom-Expanse famously advocated "silent-illumination" (默照) Ch'an: Ch'an that focuses on that direct and wordless insight, on empty-mind meditation, which he described as silently wandering the radiance of mind's boundless and formless emptiness, and there gazing into the origin of things: hence, empty-mind as the condition of awakening. This excludes all verbal teaching, of course, and it therefore follows naturally that he would demand teaching that is as direct and penetrating as possible in words, the very nature of sangha-cases and poetry.

Ch'an silent-illumination meditation is the foundation for sangha-case practice. In bare philosophical outline, such meditation begins with the practice of sitting quietly, attending to the rise and fall of breath, and watching thoughts similarly rise and fall, appearing and disappearing in a field of silent emptiness.[1] From this attention to thought's movement comes meditation's first revelation: that we are not, as a matter of observable fact, our thoughts and memories. That is, we are not that center of identity we assume ourselves to be in our day-to-day lives, that identity-center defining us as fundamentally separate from the empirical Cosmos. Instead, we are an empty awareness that can watch identity rehearsing itself in thoughts and memories relentlessly coming and going. Suddenly, and in a radical way, Ch'an's demolition of concepts and assumptions has begun. And it continues as meditation practice deepens.

With experience, the movement of thought during meditation slows enough that we notice each thought emerging from a kind of emptiness, evolving through its transformations, and finally disappearing back into that emptiness. Here we find the process of thoughts appearing and disappearing manifests Taoism's generative cosmology, reveals it there within the mind. And with this comes the realization that the cosmology of Absence and Presence defines consciousness too, where thoughts are forms of Presence emerging from and vanishing back into source-ancestral Absence, exactly as the ten thousand things of the empirical world do. That is, consciousness is part of the same cosmological tissue as the empirical world, with thoughts emerging from the same generative emptiness as the ten thousand things.

Eventually those thoughts fall silent, and we inhabit consciousness empty of all content. That is, we inhabit the most fundamental nature of consciousness itself, known in Ch'an parlance as *empty-mind* or *no-mind*. And it is mind as 無, as source-ancestral Absence—for as we have seen, that emptiness is the source of thoughts. This is to inhabit source-ancestral 無 as home-ground—dwelling that is, as we will see, the heart of sangha-case practice.[2] This empty-mind dwelling opens another dimension of awakening that is ubiquitous throughout Ch'an and *The Carefree-Ease Record*, for that empty-mind mirrors the world with perfect clarity, leaving its ten thousand things free of all thought and explanation— the sheer thusness of things utterly simple, utterly themselves, and utterly sufficient. In that empty-mind mirroring, those things become the very content of mind and identity. And in this, everyday experience becomes moment by moment another form of *carefree-ease* liberation that is central to Wisdom-Expanse's teaching in the *gathas*.

In the sangha-cases themselves, 無 functions very differently. 無 contains a double meaning that Taoism/Ch'an often exploits to great philosophical effect: in addition to "Absence," it also means "no/not." This double meaning informs a concept that explains the essence of sangha-case practice: *wu-wei* (無為). Conjured by the seminal Taoist philosophers, *wu-wei* means "not-acting," in the sense of acting without the identity-center self, or acting with an empty and therefore wild mind.

This selfless action is the movement of the Cosmos, so *wu-wei* means action integral to the Cosmos's spontaneous burgeoning forth, action *as* the Cosmos. In fact, it means acting as the very source-ancestral of the Cosmos, for in addition to "not-acting," *wu-wei* means "Absence-acting." Hence, *wu-wei* action as action directly from, or indeed, *as* the generative ontological source-ancestral: the very heart of source-ancestral dwelling.

Success in a sangha-case encounter always involves responding with this *wu-wei* spontaneity, action that lies outside logical analysis. And sangha-case teachers push students toward that goal with enigmatic utterances and outbursts and antics intended to dismantle the realm of thought that distances us from the world, to replace it with a wide-awake immediacy of experience, *carefree-ease* experience in which we move integral to the existence-tissue Cosmos. It is a dismantling of the distinctions mind creates to order the world, without which we are left with mind empty and existence a single tissue of thusness: the condition of *carefree-ease* awakening. This resolves what is the most fundamental question for Ch'an practice, and perhaps for human consciousness in general: how to move past the seeming separation between thought and silence, subjective and objective, mind and landscape, self and Cosmos.

This deconstruction is reflected in the forms of Wisdom-Expanse's teaching *gathas*. Classical Chinese poems generally have very regular forms: notably lines of uniform length—usually five or seven words—arranged in couplets. Wisdom-Expanse almost always violates this form in his *gathas*, breaking couplets and deploying lines of wildly varying lengths—a radical literary act that gives a formal representation of the demolition going on. (This can be seen in the translations, where line lengths replicate lengths in the original: not numbers of words, but relative length on the page.) Hence, an organic poetry that moves not according to rules, but with *carefree-ease* freedom.

When Ch'an teachers examined students, they looked for a student who moved in a direct and single-minded way—forceful, without self-doubt or hesitation—for that was a student who had mastered *wu-wei*. The correct response in a sangha-case encounter is whatever thought or action emerges spontaneously from that silent emptiness cultivated in meditation practice, the generative emptiness of *wu*-mind (no-mind or Absence-mind), where the logical construction of thoughts has not yet begun. This is radical self-reliance, trusting oneself rather than teachers and their words. And more radical still: it was *wu-wei* at the most profound level: "Absence-action," improvisational action in which one moves as the generative source, as the Cosmos unfurling its possibilities. And in this, it is cultivation of the sage dwelling that defines Ch'an enlightenment, *carefree-ease* dwelling heart and mind as an organic part of Tao's great transformation of things.

Such *wu-wei* responses take two forms: spoken words or physical action. When a sangha-case plays out in words, it grows directly out of the understanding of *wu-wei* gained in meditation. Rather than the calculating machinery of an isolated self, an insightful response emerges with selfless spontaneity from the empty origin-tissue: thought as Tao unfurling its transformations, or as "Absence-acting" (in contrast to the conventional idea of enlightenment as the perfection of thoughtless and tranquil emptiness). As physical action, an insightful response is selfless action integral to the unfurling Cosmos, action moving with the dynamic energy of the Cosmos. Either way, words or actions, sangha-cases are not about explaining enlightened understanding. They are, again, about *enacting* it.

And this returns us again to the *carefree-ease* of the book's title, for the term's full philosophical depth becomes clear when we remember another of Chuang Tzu's explanations: when you "move with the *carefree-ease* of Absence-action (*wu-wei*), you're stitched through the ten thousand woven things." *Carefree-ease* is, therefore, to move through life with the "profound tranquility" of the Cosmos itself as it unfurls through its perennial transformations: *wu-wei* movement in accord with the ongoing unfolding of Tao.

Carefree-ease is functionally equivalent to another concept from Chuang Tzu that recurs as a definition of sage enlightenment: *wandering boundless and free,* which was later emphasized by Kuo Hsiang, a central figure in the formation of Ch'an, who described it like this:

> The principle thought in *Chuang Tzu* is "wandering boundless and free," that liberation in Absence-action through which we find the furthest depths of self-realization.

> . . . to mount the source of heaven and earth is to abide by the original-nature of the ten thousand things, yielding and devoted as

a river. And to ride the six seasons of *ch'i*³ in their endless dispute is to wander the blur of change and transformation. If you set out like that, how could you not set out into the inexhaustible? Embrace this, mount the source of heaven and earth, depending on nothing at all—then you've mastered that wandering boundless and free, a sage of heart-sight clarity merging self and other in dark-enigma.⁴

However it's described—*carefree-ease, wandering boundless and free,* wu-wei *Absence-action*—this principle echoes down the Ch'an tradition as the essential nature of enlightened liberation: liberation not *from* this world, as in conventional Buddhism, but all the way *into* it. This attention to the very core of Ch'an culminates perhaps here in *The Carefree-Ease Record*, where it becomes the central motif of Wisdom-Expanse's teaching in the *gathas*. The image of fish drifting with *carefree-ease* recurs. Chuang Tzu's association of *carefree-ease* with both fish and dragon appears in a recurring reference to fish becoming dragons as a quasi-mythological description of enlightenment: golden-scale fish ascend cascading riverwater as a metaphor for the practice leading to enlightenment, which is likened to that fish suddenly struck by lightning and transformed into a dragon that soars up into the sky (Cases 33 and 95). And going beyond philosophical concepts to create immediate poetic evocations of the actual experience of *carefree-ease*, Wisdom-Expanse's *gathas* describe it directly over and over in a host of ways as the full realization of Ch'an awakening, as in these examples:

. . . you wander life's lazy scatter, free and easy among

spirit-lightning songs and earth-altar dances everywhere, wander clapping hands and chanting to the music's full rhythm and beat!

(8)

Liberated into the emptiness of empty skies—O—
          we soar long winds on wondrous wingbeats,
tumble through the boundless ocean of things—O—
          wander-dragons bid farewell by wild thunder!

(32)

you wander this realm alone, enlightenment seen all the way through,
wander at ease in the wild joy and delight infusing all beneath heaven.

(35)

But for all Wisdom-Expanse's flights of poetic transport, this liberation
of *carefree-ease* enlightenment is always already our everyday nature: a
steady refrain in *The Carefree-Ease Record*, and an essential element in the
original story of Chuang Tzu and the fish. Asked by a companion how he
could know the *carefree-ease* joy of fish drifting here and there in a river,
Chuang Tzu declares that he knows it simply because he is standing there
beside the river.

THE
CAREFREE-EASE
RECORD

1

World-Honored-One Ascended

One day, the World-Honored-One[5] ascended the teaching platform and sat. Sutra-Kill Manjusri,[6] regal teacher of Buddhas, sounded the announcement mallet and called out: "Behold the Dharma Emperor's dharma! Look closely! The Dharma Emperor's dharma is exactly this here before you!"

The World-Honored-One thereupon rose and descended the teaching platform.

GATHA

Can you see each wind-gust of thusness-clarity? Gossamer
mother of change, a busy shuttle working the inner-pattern's[7]

loom-of-origins weaves out the aboriginal tapestry of spring:[8]
all those secrets Lord Sun simply won't stop rising to reveal.

2

Bodhidharma Vast Expanse Absence

Southlands Emperor War-True[9] asked the Grand-Master Bodhidharma: "What is the first principle of sage reality?"

"Vast-expanse no-sage Absence,"[10] replied Bodhidharma.

"Then who is this facing me here?"

"No idea."

The emperor couldn't mirror Bodhidharma's mind. So, Bodhidharma crossed the Yangtze and made his way to Rare-Shrine Forest Monastery, where he sat facing a wall for nine years.

GATHA

Vast-expanse no-sage Absence. This magical
loom-of-origins weave itself the temple path,

success is effortless as wielding an axe without slicing your nose,
failure difficult as dropping a rice-pot without turning your head.

. He sits ice-cold in isolate quiet at Rare-Shrine Forest,
that silent darkness opening perfect insight completely:

round moon wheeling through clarities of autumn frost,
dipper trailing its night handle into Star River shallows."

Handing our robe-and-bowl devotion down boundless generations,
we've infected all heaven-and-earth with our medicine and disease.

3

East Indian Invites Patriarch

The king of an east Indian land invited the Twenty-Seventh Patriarch Prajnatara to his library. There, he asked: "Why do you never read the sutras?"

"I'm just a poor monk dwelling in Way," replied Prajnatara. "Inhaling, I don't inhabit some netherworld of *yin*-darkness. And exhaling, I don't cross a river into some plenitude of origin-tissue.[12] This is my sutra, this existence-tissue[13] world wheeling through its transformations: a hundred, a thousand, ten thousand, a hundred thousand scrolls."

GATHA

Cloud-rhino masters all glistening radiance gazing at the moon,
wood-horse masters unbridled and fast frolicking in springtime:

they have eyes cold and blue, Buddha-deep, so why struggle at
reading sutras? That's like trying to poke through tough oxhide.

Minds radiant illumination opening out limitless kalpas,
heroic strength breaking apart enemy lines, they're free:

the wordless loom-of-origins unfurls in their words all wonder

at the hinge of things. Cold Mountain followed a road up among
peaks, then forgot it. So Fathom-Gather led him back for a look.[14]

4

World-Honored-One Pointed

The World-Honored-One was out walking with the sangha. Suddenly, he pointed at the earth and said: "That's the perfect place to build a temple."

Indra, god of sky and guardian of dharma, brought a single sprout of grass and planted it there in that earth, then said: "And so, the temple is complete."[15]

The World-Honored-One's face broke into a faintly-emergent[16] smile.

GATHA

Spring blooms boundless across the hundred wildflower grasses.
Nurturing kinship with it, full of sincerity, he came and pointed,

all transformation meeting goddesses Prosperity and Destitution.[17]
The commonplace leads you by the hand into the red-dust world:

only there can empty-mind host our everyday
self, that guest emerging from outside change.

Just stop imagining great masters are somehow different than you,
then any place you are anywhere in this vast life is plenty enough.

5

Source Clearwater Rice Price

A monk asked Source Clearwater: "What is the Buddha-dharma's vast *ch'i*-weave insight?"[18]

"What is the price of rice at Black-Deer Ridge these days?" replied Source.

GATHA

Emperors who bring great peace to the world are formless.
On old farms, household customs remain pure and simple:

folks sing village songs unconcerned, drink at earth-altars.
Why should they study the virtues of legendary emperors?

6

Way-Entire Bright Dark

A monk asked Grand-Master Sudden-Horse Way-Entire: "I'm done with clever ideas like the four existential distinctions and hundred negations. Please, Master, just point directly at that *ch'i*-weave mind Bodhidharma brought from the West."

"I'm exhausted today," replied the Grand-Master. "I can't explain it for you. Go ask Wisdom-Hoard."

The monk journeyed away to ask Wisdom-Hoard, and Wisdom-Hoard said: "Why didn't you ask the master?"

"He told me to come ask you."

"I have a terrible headache today. I can't explain it for you. Go ask Hundred-Elder Mountain."

So the monk traveled to Hundred-Elder Mountain and asked. Hundred-Elder said: "I've gotten to the point that I don't understand it at all."

Finally, the monk went back to the Grand-Master and told him what had happened. The Grand-Master said: "Wisdom-Hoard's head is bright and clear. Hundred-Elder's head is dark and mysterious."[19]

GATHA

Medicine is what brings disease,
according to wise-ones long-ago,

and then disease brings doctors.
But who could cure such things?

Head bright and clear, head dark and mysterious — O —
                                        able children of our Ch'an house,
with grand precepts, without grand precepts — O —
                                        that loom-of-origins weave cut off:

they sit in Dharma Halls lopping off the mind-road and its busy tongue.
What a laugh for those ancient awl-sharp sages among the hills of India!

7

Medicine Ascended and Sat

It had been a long time since Medicine Mountain ascended the teaching platform and sat. One day, the vice-abbot spoke plainly: "Our sangha has wanted the ocean of your nurturing instruction for too long. Please, Master, talk to them about dharma."

Mountain told an attending monk to strike the bell. The sangha gathered. Mountain ascended the teaching platform and sat silent for a long time, then he descended and returned to his room. The vice-abbot asked: "Just now, you agreed to talk about dharma. So why didn't you offer even a single word of insight?"

"For sutras, there are sutra teachers. For shastras, there are shastra teachers.[20] Why are you scolding this old monk?"

GATHA

A foolish child is devoted to autumn leaves, thinking they're gold,
but a fine horse, glimpsing even a whip's shadow, chases the wind.

Thousand-year-crane moon, cloud swept through sky's boundless
emptiness: once that cold clarity's in your bones, you won't sleep.

8

Hundred-Elder Wild Fox

Often, when Hundred-Elder Mountain ascended the teaching platform, there was an old man listening. After hearing the dharma, he always left with the monks. But one day, he stayed behind. Hundred-Elder asked: "Who is this person standing here before me?"

"Someone who, in the long-lost time of Kashyapa Buddha, lived here on this mountain," replied the old man. "One day back then, a monk asked: *The great ones who have cultivated the fundamentals, who have mastered them: are they too tangled in the laws of karma?*

"*They are not tangled in karmic law,* was my answer. And since then I've been reborn five hundred times as a fox roaming the countryside. I've come to ask you, Master, if you won't please give me a hinge-phrase."

"They are not free of karmic law," Hundred-Elder replied.

And upon hearing those words, the old man had a great awakening.

GATHA

Like a foot of riverwater
or a ten-foot ocean swell,
he was reborn five-hundred times, and what could he do about it?

Not tangled in karmic law, not free of it: struggling at questions
like that, you're just thrashing your way into bramble-vine lairs.

It's such madhouse lunacy!
Can you see? Can you see?

Once you do, a newborn child's *goo-goo gaa-gaa* is explanation
enough. And you wander life's lazy scatter, free and easy among

spirit-lightning songs and earth-altar dances everywhere, wander
clapping hands and chanting to the music's full rhythm and beat!

9

Wellspring-South Chopped Kitten

One day at the monastery on Wellspring-South Mountain, monks from the eastern and western Sangha Halls were arguing over a kitten. When Wellspring-South saw this, he grabbed the kitten and held it up, saying: "If someone can say it all, say Way realized utterly, I won't chop it in two!"

No one answered. Wellspring chopped the kitten into two halves!

Later, Wellspring told his head-monk Visitation-Land what happened and asked his opinion. Visitation-Land suddenly took off his straw sandal and balanced it on his head, then walked out.

"If you'd been there," Wellspring called out after him, "that lucky kitten would have been saved!"

GATHA

Wandering cloud-and-river monks brawling between Sangha Halls:
old Wellspring-South saw through twisty thought and set it straight,

his sharp blade slicing through, butchering all possible orientation.
People have admired revered masters like this for a thousand ages,

their Ways enduring in those kindred
enough. It's like Cobra and She-Voice:

cleaving mountains to open riverbeds seaward—O—
                    for shaping the land, we honor great Emperor Cobra;[21]
smelting stone to restore sky's four directions—O—
                    for ordering the Cosmos, we esteem Lady She-Voice.[22]

In old age, Visitation-Land wandered the very edge of life,
and already, a young monk balancing that straw sandal on his head,

he was very nearly there. He was a radiant mirror among wonders,
untarnished depths this wild thusness of things all clarity-absolute.

10

Five-Terrace Shop-Woman

There was an old woman keeping shop along Five-Terrace Mountain Road. One day, a monk cultivating Presence in its every particular asked her: "Where's Five-Terrace Mountain Road?"

"Dead ahead," replied the shop-woman.

The monk started walking, but the old woman called out: "A grand teaching-monk! And still, you keep setting out like that?"

Later on, the monk told Visitation-Land about the encounter, and Land said: "Just wait. I'll go see what I can find out."

Land went and asked the same question. The next day, he ascended the teaching platform in the Dharma Hall and said to the sangha: "I questioned that old shop-woman to the very heart of it all for you, questioned her until there was nothing left to reveal."

GATHA

Whole essence mastered with age: Wellspring-South transmitted
it flawlessly, bequeathed it all to that old Buddha Visitation-Land.

Images decorate the shells of ancient turtles, so diviners kill them.
Horses out fast as the wind are soon fettered. But Land questioned

that old shop-woman's *ch'an* until there was nothing left to reveal,
then told the sangha: *thusness all clarity-absolute's no legal tender!*

11

Cloud-Gate Two Sickness

Grand-Master Cloud-Gate[23] Mountain said: "If you can't understand radiant insight through and through and then get free of it, you're stuck with two kinds of sickness. Blind to the illumination any place you wander offers, the things you face mere things: that is the first sickness. And understanding through and through, all dharmas empty, those things seeming to be mere semblance hidden among semblance: you're stuck with that too if you can't understand radiant insight through and through and then get free of it.

"Dharma-nature itself also threatens you with two kinds of sickness. To realize dharma-nature, but still cling to dharma, unable to forget it, your old ways of seeing unchanged, leaving you outside the borders of dharma-nature: that is one sickness. And to see into dharma-nature with bountiful clarity, understanding through and through, but still not liberated, still investigating in every detail the *ch'i*-breath shaping things: that too is sickness."

GATHA

The lavish fabric of these ten thousand things is a majesty of high peaks.
To understand it through and through and get free, no limits: that blinds

Buddha-eye clarity too. In the garden courtyard of a recluse, things seen
become thoughts felt. Who's strong enough to sweep the gate-path clean?

Soaked in autumn blue at the backcountry river-crossing, a boat sets out,
oars dipping into snow's sage illumination igniting silver-grass blossoms,

brocade stitched with old fishermen imagining a catch for sale at market.
A leaf tumbles and soars wind-buffeted onto waves, and then drifts there.

12

Earth-Hoard Planting Fields

Earth-Hoard Mountain asked his student, Restore Mountain: "Where have you come from?"

"From the South," replied Restore Mountain.

"What's Buddha-dharma like there nowadays?"

"There's no end of discussion and revelation, no end."

"That can't compare to what we do here, planting fields aplenty and dining on rice," said Earth-Hoard.

"But how does that help with the three realms[24] of this everyday *samsara* universe?" demanded Restore.

"Three realms of this everyday *samsara* universe?" exclaimed Earth-Hoard. "What in the world are you talking about?"

GATHA

So many ways of talking about source-ancestral: it wears you out,
words flooding mouth and ear to transmit wordless Absence-tissue.

In our household, the perennial occupation is planting fields of rice
aplenty—not glutting ourselves on talk of sages who know nothing.

Who needs to glut themselves on talk about enlightened knowing?
In the end, silver-tongued Seed-House gave up regal rank and title.

Just forget loom-of-origins insights, and set out like a bird or fish
heading home, wade recluse streamwater amid autumn-forest mist.

13

Dark-Enigma Blind Donkey

When Purport Dark-Enigma was about to pass into extinction, he gave Thrice-Sage instructions: "After I return to the great transformation of things, don't let my perfect dharma of the eye's treasure-house[25] vanish too."

"How could I ever let your perfect dharma of the eye's treasure-house vanish?" responded Thrice-Sage.

"If someone suddenly asks, how will you reveal it?"

"KHO-AAA!" shouted Thrice-Sage.[26]

"Who could have known my perfect dharma of the eye's treasure-house would vanish in this blind donkey's sophistry?"[27]

GATHA

The dharma-robe was entrusted to the Sixth Patriarch past midnight,
whipping Yellow-Plum sangha's seven hundred monks into a fury;[28]

Purport Dark-Enigma possessed his own perfect dharma of the eye,
and when it vanished with that blind donkey, people were incensed.

Their direct mind-to-mind imprint whole,
patriarchs keep transmitting the lamp, like[29]

eons leveling out oceans and high peaks,
transforming us into that Two-Moon bird.[30]

But it's altogether beyond compare, beyond a mere chatter of names.
The trick, really, is understanding how to simply take flight and soar.

14

Attendant Expanse Offered Tea

Attendant Expanse asked Heart-Sight Mountain: "All those sages from ancient times until now: where have they gone?"

"What are you doing?" demanded Mountain, "What's this game you're playing?"

"I summon forth a flying dragon-horse, the very origins of language mapped onto its back—and a lame turtle comes poking its head out!"

Mountain said nothing and left.

The next day, when Mountain left the baths, Expanse offered him some tea. Mountain gave him an affectionate slap on the back, and Expanse said: "This old bumpkin has finally gotten a first glimpse."

Mountain again said nothing and left.

GATHA

Once he came, meeting face to face, that sage-monk understood?
That's likely as a flint-spark slowly flaring into a lightning-flash!

Failing that unfurling loom-of-origins moment, he plotted deep
duplicity, trying to trick an enemy, confuse far-reaching insight,

but anything we do hits dead-center,
and who is there to deceive, anyway?

If you recognize malicious jaws jutting out — O —
                              you'll never get bamboozled,[31]
and if you perfect the gaze of Buddha-deep eyes — O —
                              you'll master effortless accord.

15

Reliance Mountain Planted Shovel

River-Act Mountain asked his student, Reliance Mountain: "Where have you just come from?"

"From the fields," replied Reliance.

"How many are there in the fields?" asked Mountain.

Reliance planted his shovel deep into the ground, then crossed his arms and stood there.

"Lots of people out cutting thatch-grass at South Mountain,"[32] said Mountain.

Reliance pulled his shovel out and walked away.

GATHA

Thinking of children and grandchildren, old masters perfected things
seen become thoughts felt. But they'd be ashamed to find what their

Ch'an household is now. Remember that talk about South Mountain,
inscribe it into your flesh and bone, and you'll repay their affections.

16

Flax-Canyon Sangha-Staff

Still an advanced monk, Flax-Canyon Mountain took up his sangha-staff and went to see Manifest-Revere. He circled around Revere's meditation-cushion three times, shook his staff once, then stood looming there before him.

"Yes, right! Right!" said Revere.

Later, Flax-Canyon traveled to see Wellspring-South Mountain. He circled around Wellspring's meditation-cushion three times, shook his sangha-staff once, then stood looming there before him.

"No, not right! Not right!" said Wellspring.

Flax-Canyon asked: "Manifest-Revere said *yes, right*, Master. Why then do you say *no, not right?*"

"Manifest-Revere may have said *Yes, right!*, but you weren't right at all. This is how storm-gales tumble you finally into ruins."

GATHA

Right or not right: better to ask if
it's osier woven into knot or bowl.

By turns revealing and concealing
master and student both struggle:

unbounded, they exhausted that wondrous and fleeting
moment. How could we equal such perfect theft: alone,

majestic heights of enlightenment in a sangha-staff shaken once,
he frolicked all idleness circling a meditation-cushion three times.[33]

In forest monasteries, confusion begins with *right* and *not right*,
yes this and *no that*. It's like dreaming up ghosts here before you.[34]

17

Dharma-Eye Hair-Width

Dharma-Eye said to his dharma-brother, Restore Mountain:

> "A hair-width distinction is error[35]
> enough to split heaven and earth.[36]

What have you understood from those lines?"
Restore Mountain answered:

> "A hair-width distinction is error
> enough to split heaven and earth."

"Fine. But what insight is there in that?" challenged Dharma-Eye.
"That's just what it's like for me," said Restore. "And you? What's it like
for you?"
Dharma-Eye replied:

> "A hair-width distinction is error
> enough to split heaven and earth."

Restore Mountain bowed reverently.

GATHA

Even a fly on the pan tips a scale out of balance. Ten thousand
generations illuminated the least discrepancy, weighed feathery

wisps to reveal the still-point. But returning home means you
throw the very gauge on our *samadhi*-still scale over into ruin.

18

Visitation-Land Dog Nature

A monk asked Visitation-Land: "A dog too has Buddha-nature, no?"

"Yes, it has,"[37] Visitation-Land replied.

"Then why's it caught in that sack of skin?"

"Must be some karmic transgression knowingly committed."

The monk began again: "A dog too has Buddha-nature, no?"[38]

"Absence," Visitation-Land replied.

"But sentient beings all have Buddha-nature," exclaimed the monk. "How could a dog not?"

"Because now you've made it into a bundle of karma-curse idea-mongering."[39]

GATHA

Yes, a dog has Buddha-nature;
no, a dog hasn't Buddha-nature:
here he dangles a hook into dark-enigma depths, looking for a fish

defying it all, a wandering cloud-and-river monk fragrant with *ch'i*.
However crystalline, explanation is just noise, noise and confusion

flooding out level and wide,
opening onto vast expanses.
Don't say our Ch'an house hasn't always been vigilant about this.

It's like the minister who presented a jade, then revealed its flaws
and stole it away. That jewel-crazed emperor understood nothing.

19

Cloud-Gate Sumeru Mountain

A monk asked Cloud-Gate Mountain: "Before even a first thought arises: can there be any error in that Absence?"

"Sumeru Mountain," replied Cloud-Gate.[40]

GATHA

Before even a first thought arises: Sumeru Mountain. Cloud-Gate
teaching dharma like that wasn't stingy about *ch'i*-weave insight:

he came at ease, offering it with both hands—but who can take it
when everyone's a pilgrim aching to venture a thousand journeys.

In this vast ocean of things,
foster white-cloud idleness:
don't open even a hair-width distinction and try to set forth there.

You can cackle like any chicken, but you'll never deceive anyone;
and you'll never enter the gateway by parroting old Bodhidharma.[41]

20

Earth-Hoard Cutting Clean

When Dharma-Eye was a traveling student, Earth-Hoard Mountain asked him: "Where are you going?"

"I'm on a pilgrimage, wandering among teachers," replied Dharma-Eye.

"What's the purpose of such a pilgrimage?" pressed Earth-Hoard.

"No idea."

"*No idea*: that's as close as we get, how we cut clean through to the intimate essence of it all," observed Earth-Hoard.

Hearing that, Dharma-Eye suddenly had a great awakening.

GATHA

Glutting yourself with studies: it's as useless now as then.
To realize *no idea*, strip the window of its curtains utterly:

stop cutting and stitching and fussing over long and short,
stop raising and lowering—make your own gaze the level.

Through dearth and plenty, our house exhausts wondrous
and fleeting moments. Walking fields, we walk fact alone.

Why thirty-year pilgrimages wandering among teachers?
Turn away and look deeply: that's clear-eyed illumination!

21

Cloud-Crag Sweeping Path

One day when he was a monk, Cloud-Crag Mountain was out sweeping the courtyard path. His friend Way-I Mountain said: "Too intent! Too fussy!"

"Watch out! Here's someone who's mastered *not intent, not fussy*!" exclaimed Cloud-Crag.

"If you are this thusness you are, simply doing what you do—then it's spring, the second moon," explained Way-I.

Cloud-Crag raised his broom into the air and said: "Which moon is this?"

Way-I fell silent and left.

Half a century later, Dark-Enigma-Sands Mountain said: "It is, without any doubt, the second moon."

And decades after that, Cloud-Gate Mountain said: "Only a slave can recognize a slave's diligence."

GATHA

Seizing the instant, one saw through Ch'an's gate with perfect clarity.
Exhausting realization and accord, the other fell silent. So, they both

charmed that Snow-Peak Mountain snake and carried it in their hands.[42]
Young, you're full of certainty. Old, you're shy about pronouncements.

22

Crag-Summit KHO-AAA!

Crag-Summit Mountain went to study under Heart-Sight Mountain. As he stepped through the courtyard gate, he paused and asked: "Who's here, simpleton or sage?"

"KHO-AAA!" shouted Heart-Sight Mountain.

Crag-Summit bowed reverently.

Hearing of this, Fathom Mountain said: "Only Crag-Summit could have done that. No one else could have made it their own and carried it forward."

"Fathom Mountain, that old bumpkin," observed Crag-Summit. "He doesn't know right-minded from wrong-headed. Meeting Heart-Sight, I revealed with one hand and concealed with the other."

GATHA

Decimating loom-of-origins
moments, you enact the very

power that keeps this grand and wondrous affair
functioning, like laws that keep a nation in order.

When self defers reverently, empty-mind thrives.
When a sovereign resents critics, advisors flatter.

Crag-Summit questioning Heart-Sight Mountain *ch'i*-weave deep:
one hand revealed, one concealed. Look! That's how mind moves!

23

Yokel-Patriarch Faced Wall

Every time he saw a monk coming, Yokel-Patriarch Mountain turned and faced a wall. Hearing of this, Wellspring-South Mountain said: "I often told him to make the emptiness that preceded kalpas his own and carry it forward, to master the wisdom that preceded Buddha's appearance in the world. But there isn't the least trace of realization in him. He is that thusness he is, simply doing what he does—and he'll keep on like that forever."

GATHA

Flavor in blandness, words said beyond
wondrous mystery become thoughts felt,

it's gossamer so unceasing it seems real—O—
                real, and yet preceding the forms of this world,
perseverance so resolute it seems obtuse—O—
                obtuse, and yet this dark female-enigma Way[43]

we treasure. Carve words into jade, and you lose its purity.
Bright in the dark abyss, a pearl's beauty is for itself alone.

Utterly dynamic and alive, *ch'i*-breath—O—
                ch'i-breath polishes sultry autumn into sheer clarity.
Idleness adrift, a thin slip of cloudline—O—
                cloudline splits asunder distances of sky and water.

24

Snow-Peak Look Viper

Instructing the assembled sangha, Snow-Peak Mountain said: "There's a turtle-nose viper on South Mountain. All of you, you really need to go take a close and careful look."

Reward-Perpetua Mountain said: "Here in this Dharma Hall, how many have lost life and fate utterly to that snake's venom?"

A monk asked Dark-Enigma-Sands Mountain about it, and Dark-Enigma-Sands said: "That's just like Reward-Perpetua. It's a start, but not how I do things."

"How would you reveal this, Master?" asked the monk.

"Why bother with South Mountain?"

Suddenly, Cloud-Gate Mountain threw his travel-staff down in front of Snow-Peak Mountain, and leapt back in fear.[44]

GATHA

Dark-Enigma-Sands Mountain rich in resolve,
Reward-Perpetua Mountain poor in audacity:

once they killed South Mountain's turtle-nose viper, what good was it?
Soaring in a wild glory of wind and cloud to meet them, dragon horns

revealed, Cloud-Gate finally appeared. Full of frolic, he threw it down,
                                        threw it down full of frolic,
and there in that sudden flash of lightning, everything was transformed.

Here at my place, I can send you wandering or summon you to practice,
but Cloud-Gate, he could take you captive and then set you utterly free.

The very heart of this grand and wondrous affair: who'll pass it on now?
Cold quiet of ancient mouths wounds you, and you never know the pain.

25

Salt-Legal Rhinoxeros[45] Fan

One day, Salt-Legal Mountain called out to the attending monk: "Bring me the fan with a rhinoxeros painted on it."

"That fan's broken," answered the attending monk.

"If the fan's broken, bring me the rhinoxeros," demanded Salt.

The attending monk had no response.

A century later, Prosper-Sustain Mountain drew an origin-mind circle[46] in the dirt, and at its center wrote the word *ox*.

GATHA

That broken fan left a tattered scatter of rhinoxeros,
and the reason for that word written in a full-round bowl of dirt.

But who can fathom a thousand years of shadow-haunted moon,
all that wondrous light elucidating each fleck of autumn wholly?

26

Reliance Mountain Pointed Snow

Reliance Mountain pointed at the snow. Then, speaking as the very Buddha-lion himself, he said: "Is there anything that surpasses the beauty of this color?"

Half a century later, Cloud-Gate Mountain said: "I would have knocked him right over into that snow!"

And a century after that, Snow-Chute Mountain said: "Old Cloud-Gate! All he could do is knock things down. He never knew how to raise things up."

GATHA

Knocked over, raised up: that Buddha-
lion there in a meditation hall of snow

averted trespass, embraced openhearted mind-ground.
And ever courageous, he saw inner-pattern Way utterly.

Crystalline radiance illuminating Buddha-deep eyes confounds home,
and lucid enlightenment turns us round until we tumble into darkness.

Seeing home clearly, patchrobe monks rely on nothing,
dwell in Absence: life and death whole,
self and other altogether unimaginable.

Splintering plum blossoms in the end with its sincere warmth—O—
                                    warmth, spring enters cold branches,
and stripping leaves scattered away with its storm-wind chill—O—
                                    chill, autumn clarifies flood waters.

27

Dharma-Eye Pointed Blinds

Dharma-Eye pointed at the blinds still down after meditation. Two monks immediately went and raised the blinds. Dharma-Eye said: "One did. One didn't."

GATHA

Pines are straight and date-brambles bent, cranes tall and ducks short.
In the days of sage-emperors, people forgot about subduing confusion:

it was a peace that kept recluse dragons at home in dark abyss,
a liberation full of ease that let birds shake off fetters and soar.

Suddenly, long-ago Bodhidharma came from the West,
and we began struggling to realize mind mirroring fact.

Tumbleweed chasing wind tumbles through emptiness,
and a riverboat going home must cut through currents:

you patchrobe monks all wild and wordless bounty, look
closely at Dharma-Eye's Lucid-Chill Mountain method.

28

Shelter-Nation Three Humilities

A monk asked Shelter-Nation: "How is it when a crane perches in a withered pine?"

"Humility of the flat ground underneath," replied Shelter-Nation.

"How is it when a drop of water freezes into a drop of ice?"

"Humility of the warm hours after sunrise."

"And when monasteries everywhere were ravaged during the Solar-Gather reign,"[47] continued the monk, "where had those benevolent Shelter-Dharma spirits gone?"

"Humility of the three-gate monastery of mountain liberation—times two."

GATHA

If you live adulthood in bitter-ice cold, autumn never bleaches your hair,
and if you live childhood without passion, you never ascend to lofty rank.

Transmit soaring thoughts crystalline pure to students? If they find streamwater to rinse ears clean of words, it's water oxherds won't let oxen drink.

29

Wind-Source Iron Ox

At the magistrate's pavilion in Altar-Evince Land, Wind-Source Mountain ascended his teaching platform in the Dharma Hall and said: "The mind-seal of patriarchs is like those huge iron-ox totems people build along rivers to ward off flooding. Lift it away quickly, and the seal remains clearly stamped. Leave it long, and the seal smears into ruins. And what if you neither lift it nor leave it? Is it the seal itself, or is it not?"[48]

At that, the venerable Black-Deer Scarp stepped forward and said: "I already possess that iron-ox totem. Who needs your seal stamped all over it?"

"I'm always fishing for great whales in these floodwaters so crystalline and vast," countered Wind-Source. "How did I catch this frog plopping around in muddy sand?"

Scarp just stood there, baffled.

"KHO-AAA!" shouted Wind-Source. "A venerable monk, and nothing to say?"

Scarp still hesitated, unsure what to do.

Swinging his abbot-staff, Wind-Source struck him a blow. Then he said: "Have you completely forgotten what we're talking about? Show me something!"

Scarp opened his mouth to speak, but Wind-Source struck him another blow.

Then the magistrate spoke up: "The dharma-law of Buddha and the dharma-law of governance—they're no different."

"What inner-pattern Way have you seen?" asked Wind-Source.

"If you don't correct when correction is needed, chaos follows."

Wind-Source descended from his seat.

GATHA

Mind-seal's like iron-ox river totems:
left long, it smears into ruins. And so:

to set out beyond, you must walk on Dharma-Nature Buddha's head,
and to come back, sit atop Transformation-Perpetua Buddha's tongue.

Wind-Source Mountain set up scales,
and Black-Deer Scarp tipped and fell:

abbot-staff blows, *KHO-AAA!* shouts,
fleeting as a flint-spark lightning-flash

life. Clear-eyed illumination detail by detail: that's the Buddha-truth
pearl posed in scale-pans, all of it slipping away in a wink of the eye.[49]

30

Tumble-Vast Kalpa-Fires[50]

A monk asked Tumble-Vast Mountain: "When the perfect understanding of kalpa-fire burns this vast thousand-Buddha-realm Cosmos down into ruins, will this unthought here-right-now also be burned down into ruins?"

"Down into ruins," replied Tumble-Vast.

"Will even thusness itself vanish away with it?"

"Away with it."

Later, the monk asked Nurture-Dragon Mountain: "When the kalpa-fire's perfect understanding burns this vast thousand-Buddha-realm Cosmos down into ruins, will this unthought here-right-now also be burned down into ruins?"

"No," replied Nurture-Dragon.

"How could that be?" asked the monk.

"Because it is itself this vast thousand-Buddha-realm Cosmos."

GATHA

Burned down not burned down:
two masters venture forth, each a thousand Buddha-realm Cosmos.

Seeing through nothing, no clarity, words only snarl you in machine-
mind tangles. It's like a life shrouded head-to-toe with bramble-vine.

Sage insight not sage insight:
to see the very heart of this grand and wondrous affair all clear-eyed

illumination, just wither away. Then without discussion or revelation,
proffer mind itself—bamboozle me, like some wily trader at market.

31

Cloud-Gate Dew Pillars

Instructing the assembled sangha, Cloud-Gate Mountain said: "Ancient Buddhas wandered among those pillars topped with bowls gathering dew in the Star River:[51] How deep into the loom-of-origins is that?"

The sangha members said nothing. Answering for them, he said: "On South Mountain, clouds rise. On North Mountain, rain falls."

GATHA

Once it flashes, primal-unity
Way's spirit-lightning blaze

is never again hidden. Beyond deepest insight, origin-tissue is and is not.
Before things seen become thoughts felt, mind-ground is there and is not.

Among confusions of wildflower blossoms on cliffwalls —O—
                              cliffwall beehives charged with honey,
and among flourishes of wild-origin grass in fieldlands —O—
                              fieldland musk-deer graced with scent:

whether from sage abbots or the Transformation-Perpetua Buddha,
enlightened illumination penetrates everywhere, magisterial as dew.

32

Reliance Mountain Mind Circumstance

Reliance Mountain asked a monk: "Where's your home?"

"Origin-Dark Land," replied the monk.[52]

"And do you often think of home?" asked Reliance Mountain.

"All the time."

"Mind is the seat of thought, and circumstance the object of thought," began Reliance Mountain. "Your home has rivers and mountains and the broad earth, towers and terraces, houses and temples, people and animals and everything else. Now, what if you turn your thought around and think down into the very foundations of mind: are all those kinds of things there?"

"When I'm in that place, I don't see such things," said the monk.

"In awakened experience, it's like that. In everyday experience, it isn't."

"Isn't there perhaps some way to explain more clearly, Master?" pondered the monk.

"More clearly, no more clearly: don't get caught there. When you're in that place, you see only primal-unity dark-enigma. So that's it: throw on some robes and sit carefree in meditation. Just stay there, simply gazing into yourself."

GATHA

No outside—and so, all embracing.
No hindrance—and so, wandering

emptiness. Within courtyard walls
like cliffs, gateway double-bolted,

we're travelers perpetually drunk on wine and sleeping soundly,
bald farmers working rich fields even though glutted with food.

Liberated into the emptiness of empty skies—O—
                    we soar long winds on wondrous wingbeats,
tumble through the boundless ocean of things—O—
                    wander-dragons bid farewell by wild thunder!

33

Three-Sage Golden Fish

Three-Sage Mountain asked Snow-Peak Mountain: "A golden-scale fish[53] escaped the net, and you still haven't said what it will eat."

"Once you've escaped that net, I'll tell you about it," replied Snow-Peak.

"Fifteen hundred students, grand master of the perfectly wise word, and not a word to say!?"

"This old monk somehow became an abbot, and that brings such tangles of trouble."

GATHA

Starting up through swelling waves,
cloud and thunder bidding farewell,
fish reveal the wondrous Buddha-Way as they leap and frolic higher,

lightning-struck in ice-cold Three-Cascade Gorge and become dragon[54]
all clear-eyed illumination. Pickle-jar no home for those golden-scale

fish, they form sanghas aging masters can't keep startling.
Face a mighty opponent long enough, and you finally forget your fear

and grow light, fluttering free and light as feathers in wind filling sails,
but no less heavy, deep and heavy as a boat so massive it barely floats.

Then, your lofty renown spanning the four seas, no one can rival you,
and you stand alone, dead-still amid gales where the eight winds meet.

34

Wind-Source Dust Mote

Teaching the assembled sangha, Wind-Source Mountain said: "We established a first dust mote, gave it a name that separated it out from the existence-tissue, and before long there was a whole nation run rampant. If we give up that dust mote, the nation vanishes away."

A century later, Snow-Chute Mountain held up his travel-staff before the assembled sangha and said: "Can any of you patchrobe monks die Wind-Source Mountain's death, live Wind-Source Mountain's life?"

GATHA

White-haired Moon-Field River fisherman become high minister
nothing like starved Solar-Summit Mountain hermits who refused:

a mere dust mote, so we distinguish among forms change unfurls.
Recluse renown, public honor: it's hard to tell true jade from fake.

35

Far-Waters Knelt Bowed

Far-Waters Mountain went to request instruction from Smuggle Mountain. He didn't bow reverently first. He simply walked straight up to the master and stood there before him.

"Just because a chicken roosts in a phoenix nest doesn't mean it's a phoenix," said Smuggle Mountain. "Go! Get out of here!"

"I've hurried on the wind from far away. Please, Master, teach me."

"There is no young-monk *you* standing here before my eyes," declared Smuggle. "And there is no old-monk *me* here either."

"KHO-AAA!" shouted Far-Waters.

"Stop!" exclaimed Smuggle. "Who needs that kind of rash and reckless frenzy? Cloud and moon are the same; stream and mountain are different. And demanding explanations from a tongueless person: that's like cutting out the tongues of everyone throughout all beneath heaven."

Far-Waters said nothing. Smuggle struck him a blow. At that, Far-Waters knelt and bowed his head to the ground.

GATHA

Live like a red-fin adrift full of contentment, rippling in the current,[55]
then you fathom it all and depend on nothing: transformed, liberated.

Once your tongue's cut out, eloquence is a mystery-art. But simply
return to your original-face, and you fathom spirit-lightning wonder:

outside meditation-hall blinds in the enlightened night—O—
                                    windblown moon radiant as midday;
littered around an age-torn tree beneath lofty cliffwalls—O—
                                    wildflowers open in perennial bloom.

Tongueless person, tongueless
person explaining the wordless
Buddha-dharma completely in a single utterance of kindred intimacy,

you wander this realm alone, enlightenment seen all the way through,
wander at ease in the wild joy and delight infusing all beneath heaven.

36

Way-Entire Was Unwell

Grand-Master Sudden-Horse Way-Entire was unwell. The abbot asked: "How are you feeling these days, Master?"

"Sun-face Buddha. Moon-face Buddha."

GATHA

Sun-face, moon-face;
star-drift, lightning-

flash quick: that image in the mirror is never you yourself.
A Buddha-truth pearl posed in scale-pans rounds on itself,[56]

and haven't you seen:
before a blacksmith's tong and hammer, there's raw hundred-fire metal,
beneath a tailor's ruler and scissors, there's a single sheet of silk whole.

37

River-Act Karma-Curse

River-Act Mountain asked his student, Reliance Mountain: "Let's say someone suddenly asks about all of us here in this sangha, wonders if we're really nothing but karma-curse idea-mongering boundless and beyond, if there's really no ancestral source-tissue root to rely on. How would you reveal the truth of this matter?"

"When monks come here," began Reliance Mountain, "I call out, *Hey you*! If they turns their heads, I say, *Yes, what is it*? Then I wait, and if they hesitate, if they pause to consider, I say: *Not only karma-curse idea-mongering boundless and beyond, but also no ancestral source-tissue root to rely on*."

"How wonderful!" exclaimed River-Act.

GATHA

If I called once and you turned your head, would you recognize
me—sometimes a luminous full moon, sometimes a thin sliver?

When your thousand-gold master drifts and crumbles away, no
path forward, silence boundless, can you find more than sorrow?

38

Dark-Enigma Thusness-Clarity

Instructing the assembled sangha, Purport Dark-Enigma said: "There is a nowhere person all thusness-clarity who is forever leaving and entering your eyes and mouths. If you're new to mind and haven't yet found direct evidence of this—Look! Look!"

A monk asked: "What is this nowhere person all thusness-clarity?"

Dark-Enigma leapt from his meditation seat and seized the monk. The monk paused to consider. Dark-Enigma pushed him away and said: "Hey, you nowhere person all thusness-clarity—what kind of dry shit-wipe stick are you?"[57]

GATHA

Delusion may be nothing like awakening,
but mysterious transmission opens clarity:

spring breaks into a hundred blooms—O—blooms in a single breath,
its new force slight as the least—O—least tug of a majestic ox team.

Tawdry mud and sand never rinse away, but clear-eyed illumination

cuts through every barrier, like an eye of pooled springwater, sweetly
bursting suddenly forth, river over its banks, flooding across the land.

39

Visitation-Land Wash Bowl

A monk asked Visitation-Land: "I've just arrived here in your thicket-forest monastery, Master. Please show me what you have to reveal."

"Have you eaten your mush?" Land asked.

"Yes."

"Then go wash your bowl."[58]

GATHA

When the mush is gone, the teaching comes: *Wash your bowl!*
Suddenly, mind and earth are of themselves in perfect accord,

a pilgrim utterly enlightened at that thicket-forest monastery.
Right now: speak up! Tell me! Is that your awakening, or not?

40

Cloud-Gate Bright Dark

Cloud-Gate Mountain asked Heaven-Peak Mountain: "Give me an answer in words."

"You still haven't arrived here before this old monk," replied Heaven-Peak.

"I'm late? What has that to do with thusness-of-itself?"

"Thusness-of-itself?" needled Heaven-Peak. "What is this thusness-of-itself?"

"They say it's bright and clear, but it's no less dark and mysterious."

GATHA

String and nock meet one another,
Indra's jewels all face one another:[59]

then a hundred arrows all hit the bull's-eye, none of them vacant,
and radiance weaves the shimmering sangha-net, never hindered.

Realize the spell deep within words that means nothing,
frolic at ease through *samadhi*'s three-shadowed earth—

and there amid the wondrous, you range through partial and whole
effortlessly, range out far and wide, wandering composed and free.

41

Far-Waters Facing Death

When Far-Waters Mountain was facing death, he called the sangha together and said: "Today, this grand and wondrous affair is itself the only issue, and I want to ask all of you about it. To affirm it is like attaching a head on top of your head, and to deny it is like searching for life by loping off your head."

At that, the head-monk said: "In green mountains, don't stop walking. In broad daylight, don't carry a lamp."

"What good's talk like that at a time like this?" demanded Far-Waters.

An elder monk named Assent-Achieve stepped forward and said: "Why ask for anything outside those two paths?"

"Not enough! Say something more."

"Whatever I say, it can't be complete," said Assent.

"I don't care if it's complete or not!" demanded Far-Waters.

"Look, I'm not some peon here for the sake of conversation!" countered Assent.

That night, Far-Waters summoned Assent-Achieve and said: "That conversation today: your words came from the very source itself! They embodied the realization our ancestral teachers offered when they said: *All this here before your eyes is not itself the dharma. And the* ch'i-*weave insight within all this here before your eyes is not the dharma of all this here before your eyes. Dharma isn't something open to eyes and ears.*

"Some words are the everyday-mind guest speaking, and some are the empty-mind host speaking.[60] If you can tell which is which, I'll transmit my alms-bowl and pilgrim-bag to you."

"I can't tell the difference," said Assent-Achieve.

"You can tell as well as I can!"

"No, I really can't tell the difference," insisted Assent.

"KHO-AAA!" shouted Far-Waters. "O what grief! What perfectly bitter grief!"

At that, a monk asked: "So what's your venerable *ch'i*-weave insight here, Master?"

"That boat of compassion ferrying the dead over into nirvana: it isn't rowed across pure waters of clarity. And that wood-goose plumb dropped to fathom watery depths: it isn't worth much in cascading gorges sliced this deep by the sword of awakening."

GATHA

Cloud for bait, moon for hook—he drifted this surging and swelling world, fishing pure waters of clarity. Old, mind all flawless solitude,

he caught nothing. Long after that suicide's "Confronting Grief" poem returned home to silence, he woke out on Flood-Gauze River, alone.[61]

42

Prajna-Devotion Water-Jar

A monk asked Nation-Teacher Prajna-Devotion: "What is the original source-tissue body of Vairocana, the Dharma-Nature Buddha?"

"Could you pass that water-jar over here?" asked Prajna-Devotion.

The monk passed the water-jar, then Prajna-Devotion said: "Okay, now put it back."

Again, the monk asked: "What is the original source-tissue body of Vairocana, the Dharma-Nature Buddha?"

"Those ancient Buddhas vanished an awfully long time ago!" replied Prajna-Devotion.

GATHA

Birds wander in sky's emptiness,
and fish dwell at home in water,

river and lake forget each other,
cloud and sky live their dreams,

but a pondering mind is merest
thread facing a thousand miles.

To know you're born all insight
and be grateful—how very rare!

43

Gauze Mountain Appearing Disappearing

Gauze Mountain asked Crag-Summit Mountain: "How is it we never stop appearing and disappearing?"

"AI-OO!" cried Crag-Summit. "Who's appearing, and who disappearing?"

GATHA

You can hack at old bramble-vine tangles
and break open tricky-fox lairs of quandary,

but a tiger can change its stripes by cloaking itself in fog,
and a dragon can change its bones by soaring on thunder.

AI-OO!
This confusion of appearance and disappearance: what kind of thing is it?

44

Solar-Burgeon Wondrous Wings

A monk asked Master Solar-Burgeon Mountain: "When Sagara the dragon-king emerges from the sea, heaven and earth rest serene. If I meet him face to face, what truth about it all will he reveal?"

"An imperial sun-bird splitting the sea open and soaring through all seed-time breath-space[62] on wondrous wings," replied Solar-Burgeon. "Who among us dares tangle with that?"

"And if I recklessly tangled with it, what would happen?"

"You would be like a pigeon attacked by a falcon," warned Solar-Burgeon. "It certainly wouldn't awaken you. Try this: just go out in front of the sangha-tower and pay close attention. That's how you'll fathom the wild thusness of things all clarity-absolute."

"If I fathom thusness-of-itself," said the monk solemnly, "I'll join hands and bow, then back away three paces."

"This right here is Sumeru Mountain[63] itself rising out of vast seas, the very center of the Cosmos! And you're such a blind tortoise! Don't wait for more teaching, more blows of my stick scarring that thick head of yours!"

GATHA

Issuing silken decrees
and shouted commands,

emperors plot within imperial walls,
and generals beyond frontier passes,

but thunder for no reason awakens the insects every spring,
and what must wind understand to dissolve drifting clouds?

That loom-of-origins weaves out gossamer skeins—O—
        skeins stitched through with gold needles and jade thread:
it's that open expanse before the earliest graph, dark—O—
        dark-enigma before even bird-track or bark-beetle script.[64]

45

Enlightenment Sutra Four Practices

The *Perfect-Enlightenment Sutra* says:

Dwell at all times without thoughts even beginning to arise, and when thoughts do arise, without trying to suppress them.

Dwell in the midst of thought without trying to understand: without understanding, you leave wild thusness itself whole.

GATHA

Majestic, lofty and majestic,
open, clear and openhearted,

sages wander a serene place
even amidst bustling clamor.

If your feet are tied with cord—cut them loose, then wander free.
If your nose is tipped with mud—rinse it clean, don't hack it off.

Why fuss and stew?
The cure is easy: it's all there on blank thousand-year-old paper.

46

Lumen-Whole Done Practicing

Instructing the assembled sangha on Heart-Sight Mountain, Grand-Master Lumen-Whole said: "Inhabit wholesale ruin—and from there, set out. Then you'll see through time itself with utter clarity, the mouths of all those ancient Buddhas tacked up on a wall. And even there you'll find someone roaring with glorious laughter. If you can recognize this person—you're done studying, done practicing."

GATHA

Harvest!
Scythe down your majesty. Scatter it

where cloud winnows and wind mills.
In this river of fate, water cold amidst

autumn skies, brocade-bright fish frolic perfectly delectable:[65]
to catch them all, just dangle a single hook of crescent moon.

47

Visitation-Land Cypress Tree

A monk asked Master Visitation-Land: "What is the *ch'i*-weave mind Bodhidharma brought from the West?"

"That cypress tree in our courtyard," replied Land.[66]

GATHA

Eyebrow a shore crossing snow
and eye a river holding autumn,

mouth a lake drumming waves
and tongue a boat riding rapids,

hand sweeping away confusion,
shit-wipe stick conjuring peace

vast and carefree: that's old-man Visitation-Land
stirring up thicket-forest monasteries even after death took him.

Diligent practice? You'll only build a cart that follows old ruts.
And Absence-root teaching just clogs ditches and chokes drains.

48

Vimalakirti Dharma-Gate Nonduality[67]

Vimalakirti asked Sutra-Kill Manjusri, regal teacher of Buddhas:[68] "How does a bodhisattva pass through the dharma-gate of nonduality?"

"Here's my guess about these dharma-realm expanses,"[69] replied Manjusri. "No words and nothing said. No teaching and nothing learned. Free of questions and free of answers. That's how you pass through the dharma-gate of nonduality."

Then Manjusri asked Vimalakirti: "But we each say it in our own way. How would you say it? How does a bodhisattva pass through the dharma-gate of nonduality?"

Vimalakirti fell silent, shadowy and silent.

GATHA

Manjusri asked old Vimalakirti how to cure the disease, how to
open the gate of nonduality and make sight itself into our home.

Fake jade outside, pure and true inside: don't say which is real.
Act free of cause and consequence, and you're done with regret.

When that guy presented a jewel rough outside but pure—O—
                pure and true inside, emperors cut off his legs for fraud,
and when that noble healed a wounded snake, shimmering—O—
                shimmering it brought him that perfect pearl as reward:

but what can metaphor explain?
And why look for flaws in jade?
Everyday life, and dark Absence whole: they aren't far apart at all.

49

Fathom Mountain Altar Offerings

Fathom Mountain made offerings at the altar beneath a portrait[70] of his teacher, Cloud-Crag Mountain. Then he spoke to the sangha about how Cloud-Crag was himself utter and wild thusness all clarity-absolute.

A monk asked: "When Cloud-Crag Mountain said *Simply this! This right here!*, what was his wordless *ch'i*-weave insight?"

"At the time, I almost failed to see it," replied Fathom Mountain.

"I wonder if Cloud-Crag himself understood," mused the monk.

"If he didn't understand," observed Fathom, "how could he explain thusness-of-itself so clearly? And if he did understand, how could he even try to talk about such thusness?"[71]

GATHA

How could he explain thusness-of-itself so clearly:
rooster crowing in the fifth watch, sunrise over houses and forests?[72]

How could he even try to talk about such thusness:
moon pure as a thousand-year crane nesting in cloud-swept pines?

Radiant clarity, mind awake mirrors these ten thousand things and
existence-tissue whole, enlightenment any loom-of-origins season

itself. Gateway wind, our practice awakens expanses — O —
                    expanses where its pattern wanders gossamer on and on,
teacher opening into student, continuing transformed — O —
                    transformed where insight blazes boundless and beyond.

50

Snow-Peak What's This

When Snow-Peak Mountain was living at the shrine-hut, two monks came to offer bows in reverence to him. When he saw them coming, Snow-Peak pushed the courtyard gate open, leaned out, and said: "What's this?"

One of the monks said the same thing back: "What's this?"

Snow-Peak bowed slightly and went back inside.

Later, that monk went to visit Crag-Summit Mountain.

"Where have you just come from?" asked Crag-Summit.

"From Summits-Pass South."

"Did you visit Snow-Peak Mountain there?"

"Yes."

"What's he teaching people these days?"

The monk told Crag what had happened, and Crag asked: "So, what did he say?"

"Nothing. He just bowed slightly and went back inside the shrine-hut."

"Ah, well. When I saw him, I didn't explain all the way beyond a last ever utterance. If I had, no one in all beneath heaven could rival old Snow-Peak."

At the end of the summer session, the monk asked again about Snow-Peak, hoping to understand more deeply.

"Why didn't you ask the first time?" wondered Crag-Summit.

"I knew it wasn't easy, and I didn't want to pry."

"Snow-Peak and I share this one lineage, but we won't die in the same lineage. If you want to understand all the way beyond a last ever utterance, it's *Simply this! This right here!*"

GATHA

To cut and polish us jade-pure, teachers
tell tales about the forms change unfurls:

staff thrown into a lake becoming dragon and setting out;
shuttle asleep on a wall becoming dragon and soaring up.

How many—O—how very many share this one lineage,
but how few—O—how very few die in the same lineage:

beyond a last ever utterance, *Simply this! This right here*:
windblown boat ferrying the moon clear across autumn lakewater!

51

Dharma-Eye Boat Land

Dharma-Eye asked elder-monk Awaken: "Did you come by boat or by land?"

"By boat," replied Awaken.

"And where's the boat?"

"Sunk in the river."

After Awaken left, Eye asked a monk standing nearby: "Tell me: that monk who was just here—did he possess the Buddha-deep dharma-eye's clarity whole, or didn't he?"

GATHA

Water can't clean water any cleaner,
and gold can't purify gold any purer.

A horse changing color: who can see its abiding nobility?
And a *ch'in* without strings: who can delight in its music?[73]

Before words, before trigrams and knotted cords: that's all lost now,[74]
and that thusness-clarity mind of a primordial Swirl-Roam Cosmos.[75]

52

Twofold Mountain Dharma Body

Master Twofold Mountain asked the venerable Heart-Sight Mountain: "Buddha's thusness-clarity dharma-nature: it's exactly like the emptiness of empty skies. It reflects the shimmering appearance of each particular thing—like a moon in water. How would you explain the inner-pattern Way of such reflecting?"

"Donkey peering into a well," replied Heart-Sight.

"Your words have spread Way out nicely in the sun," said Twofold Mountain, "but that's only 80 percent."

"And you, Master, how would you say more?"

"Well peering into a donkey," answered Twofold.

GATHA

Donkey peering into well,
well peering into donkey:

this wisdom enfolds Absence and beyond
to clarity suffusing the bounty of Presence.

Decipher Buddha-nature talismans hidden under robes?
You won't find any books in our household—just that

threadless loom-of-origins. There, shuttle weaving out the spangled
grain of things far and wide, *ch'i*-mind reveals its every possibility.

53

Yellow-Bitterroot Nibbling Dregs

Instructing the assembled sangha, Yellow-Bitterroot Mountain said: "You're oafs like all the rest, nibbling at stale wine-dregs. If you keep up your traveling-pilgrim nonsense, where will you find anything like this very today? Don't you know there isn't a single Ch'an teacher anywhere in the whole empire?"

A monk leapt forward to interrupt: "What!? But there are people everywhere nurturing disciples and leading sanghas. So what are they revealing?"

"I didn't say there's no Ch'an, just that there are no teachers."

GATHA

Mountain trails divide into dyed threads, hard work to follow through
thick leaves and crowded blossoms. It's the ruins of ancient patriarchs:

how wondrous! Here, you can master those levers Changemaker pulls,[76]
wander a vessel of cloud and river shaped on the Great Potter's wheel,[77]

slice away the tangles of delusion,
shear the wool of self and dharma.

Scale-bar gauge, exquisite mirror,
jade-pure ruler, golden blade: old

Yellow-Bitterroot parsed things to an autumn hair's-breadth,
sat all stillness scything spring wind, no deep-sky liberation anywhere.

54

Cloud-Crag Great Compassion

When they were monks together, Cloud-Crag Mountain asked Way-I Mountain: "What does that Bodhisattva of Great Compassion do with all those hands and eyes?"

"It's like someone in the night groping behind them for a pillow," replied Way-I.

"I understand."

"How would you reveal your understanding?" asked Way-I.

"My body is everywhere altogether hands and eyes."

"You've spread Way out vast and perfectly apparent in the sun!" exclaimed Way-I. "Still, that's just 80 percent."

"And how would you reveal it, Teacher?" asked Cloud-Crag.

"My body is through-and-through hands and eyes."

GATHA

Empty-mind opens so far and wide all
eight directions seem a grated window.

Spring enters earth's music of seasons without form or self.
Moon drifts deep-sky emptiness without pause or hindrance.

Clarity-jewel eyes, Prosperity and Destitution goddess arms:[78]
how can some fantasy body compare to this body right here,

these hands and eyes manifesting the loom-of-origins whole?
And aren't our words, too, wondrous Buddha-Way distances?

55

Snow-Peak Head-Cook

Snow-Peak Mountain was working as head-cook at Mirror-Sight Mountain. One day, he was running late with a meal. Abbot Mirror-Sight Mountain nestled his bowls in hand and set out for the dining hall. As he passed the Dharma Hall, Snow-Peak called out to him: "Old man! No bell announced mealtime, no drum called: where are you going with those bowls?"

Mirror-Sight returned to his rooms.

Later, Snow-Peak told Crag-Summit what had happened, and Crag said: "Even with all his disciples great and small, Mirror-Sight hasn't understood all the way through to a last ever utterance."

When he heard about this, Mirror-Sight Mountain sent his attendant to summon Crag-Summit and asked: "So you don't approve of this old monk?"

Crag-Summit told him what he thought.

Mirror-Sight gave in and walked away. But the next day, when he ascended the teaching platform in the Dharma Hall, he was through-and-through transformed. Nothing like what he was before.

Clapping his hands together and laughing wildly, Crag-Summit called out: "It's amazing, old man! You've done it, understood all the way beyond a last ever utterance! In all beneath heaven, there's no one can rival you now!"

GATHA

Understanding all the way beyond a last ever utterance: it's Absence
wherein parent and child blurred so utterly at Mirror-Sight Mountain.

That southland sudden-awakening sage always visits when a sangha[79]
sits empty, still. So why cackle at them like some mountain partridge?

56

Spirit-Lightning White Rabbit

Spirit-Lightning Mountain and Fathom Mountain were out walking together. Suddenly, a white rabbit went bounding away in front of them. "How perfectly marvelous!" exclaimed Spirit-Lightning.

"What did you see there?" asked Fathom.

"A white-robed commoner become high minister."

"Old and wise, vast and deep—and still, you talk like this?"

"Okay, so what did you see there?" asked Spirit-Lightning.

"After many generations of high ministers, a family fallen for now into poverty."

GATHA

Live strong as frost and snow,
walk serene as mist and cloud.

Some leave the country to live
free, and some cross a bridge,

some plot and plan to found new dynasties, and some avoid
even noble emperors. Alarmed by both renown and disgrace,

you can trust yourself utterly, join fish-and-firewood villagers,
mind become this wild thusness of things all clarity-absolute.

57

Solar-Strict One Thing

When he was a student, Solar-Strict Mountain asked Visitation-Land: "That one primal-unity thing: I can't bring it with me here. What shall I do?"

"Throw it away!" replied Visitation-Land.

"If I can't bring it with me," puzzled Solar-Strict, "how can I throw it away?"

"Alright then, take it and go!"

GATHA

Not ready for subtle strategies, he's ruined on the first move.
Awakened of itself, ordinary mind avoids sparring with sages,

smashes the game-board, axe-handle too broken into pieces.[80]
Rinse everyday nature pure, and you wander like mountains.

58

Diamond Sutra Worthless Bonehead

The *Diamond Sutra* says: *If someone derides you as a worthless bonehead, it's because the sins they committed in a previous life pitched them into evil ways. Once you realize this, you're free.*

GATHA

On and on through highs and lows,
karmic cause-and-effect confusion,

why chase far and wide after that person you face in the mirror,
or smash a village oven open with your staff to set its god free?[81]

Smash an oven wide open,
exalt facts themselves seen,

or just say
that's how I've always turned my back on myself.

59

Azure-Forest Dead Snake

A monk asked Azure-Forest Mountain: "What happens when a student takes a shortcut?"

"There's a dead snake on the main road," replied Forest. "Don't get anywhere near its head."

"What happens if I get close to its head?" wondered the monk.

"You lose your root in the grand unfurling of things, your very nature, your life."

"And if I stay away?"

"There's no avoiding that snake, no matter where you go," replied Forest.

"If that's true, what can I do?"

Forest paused for a moment, then confided: "It's vanished now, gone completely!"

"I wonder where it's gone?" asked the monk, playing along.

"Into grasses so deep no one can search there."

"You'd better be careful, Master," taunted the monk, "or you'll find yourself in the midst of those very grasses!"

Forest clapped his hands together and exclaimed: "Ahh—first-rate snake venom!"

GATHA

When three-elder darkness swings the rudder,
night's lone boat wheels around toward home,

autumn river a single current of flowing mist,
silver-grass blossoms snowing on both banks.

Wind strong in the sails, no one there rowing, it glides on and on,
flute-song calling the moon down among recluse island expanses.

60

Iron-Grinder Water-Buffalo

When Iron-Grinder stopped at River-Act Mountain, Mountain said: "Venerable Water-Buffalo, you've come!"

"Tomorrow, our vast sangha gathers on Lookout-Terrace Mountain for the seclusion-fast,"[82] she announced. "It's only a thousand miles away. Are you going?"

River-Act Mountain lay down and stretched out for a nap.

Iron-Grinder went on her way.

GATHA

It takes a hundred battles won to arrive carefree in venerable old-age?
Why not roam lazybones days, and ditch that struggle to master it all?

It's like ranging wide on a gold horse with a jade whip: just wander
life all idleness, rich with luminous moonlight and crystalline wind.

61

Heaven-Peak Single Path

A monk asked Heaven-Peak Mountain: "For holy Buddhas everywhere throughout all ten distances of time and space, there's a single path entering the gate of nirvana. But I can't find that Buddha-Way path anywhere."

Peak scratched a single line in the dirt with his travel-staff—primal-unity line, horizon line that first separated heaven and earth[83]—then said: "It's right there!"

Later on, the monk told Cloud-Gate Mountain what had happened and asked him about it. Cloud-Gate said: "This fan leaps out into Thirty-Three-Peak Heaven, to lofty Sumeru Mountain at the very center of the Cosmos,[84] where it slaps Lord Sakradevanam Indra's nose.[85] And if someone takes a stick and even so much as touches a carp in the eastern sea, rain pours down by the bucketful! Understand? Understand?"

GATHA

Burning herbs can't cure a dead horse. If you think sitting still
amid altar incense returns anyone to life, you're in deep trouble.

You can toil away life, sweat from every pore, or trust the way
Ch'an peels eyelids away, revealing awakened sight wide open![86]

62

Mongrol-Grain Awakening Vanished

Mongrol-Grain told a monk to go ask Reliance Mountain: "Can people these days still find awakening?"

"It isn't that awakening has vanished," answered Reliance. "But once you've fallen into everyday mind, what can you do?"

The monk returned to Mongrol-Grain and delivered Reliance Mountain's answer. Mongrol gave his deep approval.

GATHA

Everyday mind is only partial: it's always trying to capture reality.
Awakening shatters delusion, jettisons fish-traps and rabbit-snares.[87]

Insight—O—you'll grow webbed toes before you master insight.
And understanding wisdom is like biting your navel: impossible.

Full-moon ancient and bitter-ice cold, autumn weeping silent dew;
birds perched in jade-pure forests frosty, and dawn winds wintry:

that's the sheer clarity grand old Reliance Mountain bequeathed us,
utterly flawless and without scar, a white-jade amulet to treasure.

63

Visitation-Land Asked Death

Visitation-Land asked Dice-Thrown Mountain: "After dying utterly to this world, mind exquisitely vacant, the Great Death—how is it when a person comes back to life?"

"You needn't travel by night," replied Dice-Thrown, "to arrive in the thrown enlightenment of morning."

GATHA

Cities overgrown by weeds, rock timeless: mystery ends and begins,
and at the empty center of things, sight illuminates vast expanses of

emptiness. So you needn't travel by night to arrive in dawn's thrown
radiance. It's just that no one trusts geese and fish to teach us Ch'an.

64

Adept-Beckon Transmission Continues

Head-monk Adept-Beckon asked Dharma-Eye: "Now that you've founded your own monastery, whose transmission continues in you?"

"Earth-Hoard Mountain's," replied Dharma-Eye.

"So you've turned your back on Reward-Perpetua Mountain, your primary teacher?"[88]

"Reward-Perpetua had one hinge-phrase, and I never understood it."

"Why didn't you ask?" wondered Adept-Beckon.

"*The one body all ten thousand things disclose*: how would you reveal the *ch'i*-deep insight in that?"

Adept-Beckon raised his Buddha-whisk straight up.

"That's what I learned at Reward-Perpetua's place," said Eye. "But what about you, how would you reveal it?"

Beckon kept silent.

"That seems exactly like the one body all ten thousand things disclose — but are you casting the ten thousand things aside, or holding them close?"

"Holding them close."

"Both!" cried Eye.

And monks on every side of the room shouted: "You're casting them aside too!"

Dharma-Eye added: "The one body all ten thousand things disclose! That! Just that!"

GATHA

Thought ended, you're Buddha gazing. This
world of dust laid bare, you're free of sutras.

That's how our household dharma shimmers,
and then, who are you at this courtyard gate?

Moon follows a boat sailing riverwater's bleached-silk clarities,
spring scatters blazing scars of wildflower bloom across greens:

casting aside or holding close?
Listen, listen to that challenge!

Lumen-Abyss returned home to realization and three overgrown[89]
garden paths. His pine and chrysanthemum: they're fragrant still.

65

First Mountain Young Bride

A monk asked First Mountain: "What is Buddha?"
  "Young bride riding a donkey led by her age-worn mother-in-law."

GATHA

Young bride riding a donkey led by her age-worn mother-in-law:
unassuming as wind, it's occurrence-appearing-of-itself realized.[90]

Neighbor girls watch, faces wrinkled scowls: you have to laugh!
Onlookers only deepen their ugliness, never blossom into beauty.

66

Nine-Peak Beginning End

A monk asked Nine-Peak Mountain: "What is the beginning?"

"Eyes wide open, but not awake enough to see the dawn sun rising," replied Nine-Peak.

"What is the end?" continued the monk.

"Not sitting on the ten-thousand-year meditation-cushion."

"How about when there's a beginning but no end?"

"The whole time, nothing treasured," said Nine-Peak.

"And when there's an end but no beginning?"

"Well-fed, no strength."

"So then what is it when you see with utter clarity how beginning and end are in perfect accord, how they are together whole?" asked the monk.

"Children and grandchildren bodying forth a force we can't understand here in this room full of talk."

GATHA

Compass for circles, square for lines,
whether out for work or stored away.

Stunned and stumbling, a bird shelters among silver-grass.
Caught in a hedge, a goat tries to back out or push through.

Dinners out at other people's houses,
sleeping always back home in yours,

dark clouds swell and let loose rain,
glistening dew freezes into icy frost:

it's all jade-pure thread cascading together through the eye of a needle,
silk brocade ceaselessly spilling forth from the heart of a loom-shuttle.

In a woman barren as stone, that loom-of-origins stops dead—O—
                         dead where night's blackness opens toward midday,
and in a man witless as wood, the Buddha-Way swerves back—O—
                         back where moon-shadow wanders every resolution.

67

Garland Sutra *Prajna*-Wisdom

The *Flower-Garland Sutra* says: "Now I understand how all sentient beings everywhere possess the *prajna*-wisdom of Buddha Existence-Tissue Arrival[91] and see with his heart-sight clarity, how only the attachments of thought keep us from direct realization of that."

GATHA

Heaven sheltering, earth bearing up,
this mighty mudball of a world, this

dharma-realm: embrace it whole, and you're boundless;[92]
dissect it down into emptiness, and you've lost the inner.

All dark-enigma, shadow-emergent
coming and going indistinguishable,

Buddhas and patriarchs only appear because they're paying word-
karma debts. Just ask that old master Wellspring-South Mountain,

he'll tell you: you're better off just gnawing on a leaf of cabbage.

68

Stealth Mountain Swings Sword

A monk asked Stealth Mountain: "What's it like when you cut through the dust of this world and see Buddha?"

"You just have to swing the sword," replied Mountain. "And if you don't, you're like a fisherman perched high in a nest."

The monk went and asked Stone-Frost Mountain: "What's it like when you cut through the dust of this world and see Buddha?"

Stone-Frost answered: "There are some without a homeland, nowhere they belong: where will you meet them?"

When the monk returned, he asked Stealth Mountain about Stone-Frost's answer. Stealth Mountain ascended the Dharma Hall and said: "For our Ch'an household's teaching and practice, Stone-Frost can't compare to this old monk. But for profound words that lead deep into the inner-pattern, he's a hundred steps beyond me."

GATHA

Awesome *ch'i*-sword sweeping stars and rinsing armies clean,
stilling confusion, bringing realization home: isn't it you, you

clearing dawn haze, leaving skies crystalline to the four seas,
you Lord Change all Absence-action trailing out regal robes?

69

Wellspring-South Water-Buffalo

Instructing the assembled sangha, Wellspring-South Mountain said: "All those Buddhas across time's three realms of past, present, and future: none of them understood existence-tissue Presence itself. But black otters and white water-buffalo, they understand perfectly.

GATHA

Crippled and lame, we scuttle and shamble,
ragged and bedraggled, we tear and tatter—

but if you stop grasping at this wild world,
each and every thing is unbearable clarity.

Shadowy, shadowy and silent—mind knows its own fieldland calm.
Rising, rising and soaring—who says filling the belly is foolhardy?

These dharma-realm expanses are themselves the banquet. Original-
face downcast, scouring teachings: you never eat your fill like that!

70

Tribute Asked Original-Nature

When they were head-monks, Tribute Mountain asked Restore Mountain: "How can I know with enlightened clarity how to bring unborn original-nature to life, bring it to life and make it last?"

"Shoots grow into the utter enlightenment of bamboo," replied Restore. "If you hack it up and use it for splints, what's left of that realization?"

"Someday, you'll awaken to yourself and dwell in that awakening."

"This simply is what I am," ventured Restore. "And you? What wordless *ch'i*-weave insight are you revealing here?"

"This is where the manager works so our monastery keeps running. And that's where the cook works so we can eat."

Restore Mountain bowed reverently.

GATHA

Expansive, alone, depending on nothing,
all unfettered and magisterial in idleness:
this homeland is tranquil, but sages like that are few and far between.

The feeble-minded chase enlightenment by degrees, in fits and starts,
but body wild and mind vast, you simply give up *yes this* and *no that*,

and *yes this, no that* given up,
you stand isolate on this earth among the wheel-ruts of Absence itself.

71

Kingfisher-Cliff Mountain Eyelids

Instructing the assembled sangha at the end of summer session, Kingfisher-Cliff Mountain said: "I've been here all summer for you, my friends. I've talked and talked. Now, look closely at this Kingfisher-Cliff: am I blinded by eyelids pinched closed?"[93]

"It takes an empty mind to be a thief," observed Prosper-Nurture Mountain.

"Revealed," quipped Reward-Perpetua Mountain.

"Gateway," declared Cloud-Gate Mountain.[94]

GATHA

Mind of a thief perfected,
and gall of a sage—they
face this loom-of-origins far and wide, detail by detail, in gratitude:

old Prosper-Nurture and Cloud-Gate
revealing original-nature even through lips that lie,

Kingfisher-Cliff and Reward-Perpetua
peeling eyelids away, illuminating wide-open eyes.

Is there no end to uptight
Ch'an adepts yammering

on and on about
ending words and even *ch'i*-weave meaning itself?

Digging themselves into graves, they
swill down *ch'i*-power, wolf down wise teachings;

and tangling long-ago ancestors, they
sit facing walls, scamper around clapping clappers.

72

Bull's-Eye Altar Monkey

When he was a student, Reliance Mountain asked Bull's-Eye Altar: "What is the inner-pattern Way of Buddha-nature?"

"Let's try an allegory," began Bull's-Eye Altar. "It's like putting a monkey in a room with six windows. Someone outside calls, *Chimp! Chimp!*, and the monkey answers. That's like all six windows calling and all six windows answering."

"Only if the monkey's dozed off. Care to try another explanation?"

"Bull's-Eye bounded from his meditation-cushion, seized Reliance and said: "Chimp me and chimp you are looking at each other right here!"

GATHA

Chill sleep in a snowbound house: the year's fallen into ruins,
shadowed mystery. My overgrown gate stays closed. I watch

cold and withered garden trees reveal the unfurling of change.
Spring wind comes again, stirs the poem's ashes up into flight.

73

Twofold Mountain Done Honoring

A monk asked Twofold Mountain: "How is it you're not wearing ancestral Buddha-robes?"

"I'm done honoring ancestors," replied Twofold Mountain.

"And what's it like now that you're done honoring ancestors?"

"I love getting topsy-turvy drunk."

GATHA

A Ch'an household has no neighbors. Courtyard and gate crystalline-
pure, you spend years sweeping the gateway clean. No trace of dust,

transformed by radiant illumination into tumbled ruins of moonlight,
it's a place to dwell before calendars and hexagrams cut things apart.[95]

Done honoring ancestors,
you walk out into spring,
wander wine-ignited and singing wildly, robes falling open and away,

hair all chaos. At ease and carefree, no idea who's who, you're topsy-
turvy drunk, the vast tranquility of Absence your only business now.

74

Dharma-Eye Natureless Nameless

A monk asked Dharma-Eye: "In the teachings, it is said: *All dharmas are made of Absence dwelling within source-tissue origins.*⁹⁶ What is *Absence dwelling within source-tissue origins?*"

"Before the ten thousand forms emerge, the natureless," replied Eye. "And before the ten thousand names arise, the nameless."

GATHA

Leaving no trace
and no news ever,

white cloud drifts rootless and free,
and what color is crystalline wind?

Scattering all *yang*-deep heaven shelters, you realize no-mind,
holding all *yin*-deep earth supports, you realize great strength:[97]

then you can fathom the dark-abyss source of a thousand ages
and manifest the germinal pattern of these ten thousand things.

Monastery-and-market sangha-gathering: this world
is Samantabhadra Buddha's purity;[98]

gate standing open atop the sangha-tower: that space
is Maitreya Buddha's paradise time.[99]

75

Perennial Inner-Pattern Talisman

When he was a student, Crag-Talisman Mountain asked Crag-Summit Mountain: "What is the source-tissue root's perennial inner-pattern?"

"Move!" shouted Crag-Summit.

"And if I move, what is it then?"

"You don't understand it at all, that source-tissue root's perennial inner-pattern."

Talisman just stood there, baffled. So Crag-Summit whispered: "If you move, you're not yet free from life's dusty confusions. And if you don't move, you're forever mired in birth and death."[100]

GATHA

A Buddha-truth pearl needs no dragon den,[101]
and a great jewel needs no polishing. Sage[102]
masters of Way treasure snags too in this world Absence unfurls.

Move, don't move: toss all that out, and life's dusty confusion is
empty. Then you depend on nothing, dwell alone, lofty and free.

76

First Mountain Three Times

Instructing the assembled sangha, First Mountain said: "Old masters say that if a teacher must explain only once before you come to realization, you'll be the teacher of Buddhas and patriarchs. If a teacher must explain a second time, you'll be the teacher of all heaven and earth. And if it takes three times, you'll never rescue even yourself."

A monk asked: "How many times did your teacher explain before you were realized, Master?"

"In the third watch,[103] as the moon set, I threaded my way alone through the market."

GATHA

Skulls of Buddhas and patriarchs strung on a single thread: it's our
steady arrow of silent transmission, waterclock deep and profound,

this loom-of-origins world deep and heavy as a boat so massive it
barely floats, cloud-armies ablaze with flights of lightning frenzy.

Here in our household, gazing into the great transformation,
you recognize the worthless as precious, the precious as worthless,

realize the Buddha-truth pearl. Then you're perfectly formless — O —
                              formless and empty Way so gossamer on and on,
Absence-cleaver adrift and wandering this lost ox of a world — O —
                              world all heart sliced into slab after bloody slab.

77

Reliance Mountain Well Enough

A monk asked Reliance Mountain: "Can you still decipher written words, Master?"

"Well enough," replied Mountain.

The monk then walked a single circle to the right around Reliance Mountain and said: "What word is this?"

Mountain wrote the word *ten* on the ground: 十.

The monk walked a single circle to the left around Reliance Mountain and said: "Then what word is this?"

Mountain changed 十 into the sacred word *auspicious ten-thousand*: 卍.

The monk thereupon scrawled an origin-mind circle[104] on the ground and with both hands raised it over his head, like a demon colossus wielding sun and moon in all their wild *ch'i*-origin power. Then he said: "What word is *this*?"

In response, Mountain scrawled an origin-mind circle around the 卍 graph.

At this, the monk struck the pose of a thunderbolt Buddha wild too with *ch'i*-origin power.

"That's it!" cried Mountain. "That's it exactly! You've taken such good care of it all!"

GATHA

The gaping ring of Way's empty sky is never filled.
Words carved into the emptiness seal have no form.

On earth's pivot, heaven wheels wondrous mystery.
Threads of war and culture weave fabric of silence.

Cleave it all apart or knead it whole,
stand alone or set out together where

loom-of-origins reveals the dark-enigma hinge—O—
                    hinge deep as lightning amid clear blue skies,
where eyesight harbors tranquil-deep radiance—O—
                    radiance deep as stars seen in broad daylight.

78

Cloud-Gate Gruel-Cake

A monk asked Cloud-Gate Mountain: "What is small-talk that surpasses Buddhas and transcends patriarchs?"

"Gruel-cake," replied Cloud-Gate.[105]

GATHA

Gruel-cake as the small-talk surpassing Buddhas and patriarchs:
understood clear through, that counsel is altogether flavorless.

You patchrobe monks: one day, you'll realize your belly's full
and know Cloud-Gate's original-face is no other than your own.

79

Perpetua-Sands Step Beyond

Perpetua-Sands sent a monk to ask Master Gather: "How was it before you met Wellspring-South Mountain?"

Gather was silent for a long time. At last, the monk asked: "What about after you met him?"

"There is nothing else," replied Gather.

The monk returned to Perpetua-Sands and told him what had happened. Perpetua-Sands said:

If you sit grounded in meditation atop the dharma-talk flagpole,[106] you've begun. But it's far from clarity-absolute. A thousand feet

up on that flagpole, at the top, step out beyond—then you'll see these ten distances of time and space are your entire self whole.

The monk asked: "On top of the dharma-talk flagpole, a thousand feet up, how do you step out beyond?"

"Mountains of Lucid-Land," replied Perpetua, "rivers of Revere-Land."

"I don't understand," said the monk.

"Everything between the four seas, this entire five-lakes world: it's all the great transformation of Wellspring-South Mountain unfurling his own nature."

GATHA

A simple rooster-crow shatters dreams of carving the perfect jewel.
Gaze in wonder, and everything everywhere is equivalent in beauty.

Because they're all sincerity, wind and thunder rouse spring insects;
because they're so perfectly wordless, peach and plum make a path.

When the season comes, use its strength to plow and plant:
forget fears of sinking knee-deep into the mud of springtime fields.

80

Dragon-Fang Passed Clapper

When he was a student, Dragon-Fang Mountain asked Kingfisher Shadowed-Emergence:[107] "What is the *ch'i*-weave mind Bodhidharma brought from the West?"

"Pass me that clapper to announce meditation," said Shadowed-Emergence.

Dragon-Fang handed the wooden clapper to Shadowed-Emergence, who swung it and struck Fang a blow.

"You can strike me all you want," hissed Dragon-Fang. "But there's still no *ch'i*-weave mind for Bodhidharma to bring from the West."

Traveling years later, after his awakening under Fathom Mountain, Dragon-Fang asked Purport Dark-Enigma: "What is the *ch'i*-weave mind Bodhidharma brought from the West?"

"Pass me that meditation-cushion," replied Dark-Enigma.

Dragon-Fang passed the cushion to Dark-Enigma, who swung it and struck Fang a blow.

"You can strike me all you want," cackled Dragon-Fang. "But there's still no *ch'i*-weave mind of Bodhidharma."

Dragon-Fang eventually became an abbot, and a monk asked: "Back in the years when you asked Shadowed-Emergence and Dark-Enigma about Bodhidharma's *ch'i*-weave mind, did those two awakened sages illuminate enlightenment?

"You can illuminate enlightenment all you want," replied Dragon-Fang, "but there's still no *ch'i*-weave mind of Bodhidharma."

GATHA

Facing meditation clapper and cushion, Dragon-Fang is home
everywhere here in this loom-of-origins weave of occurrence.

No *ch'i*-weave mind, you're stripped bare, enlightened eye lit
and so wide-open it seems you're drifting that far edge of sky.

No sword of insight hangs in empty-sky emptiness,
but you can float the Star River on a wandering raft,[108]

hide stampeding elephants in wild-origin grass nearing spring,
reveal writhing snakes in the basket of mind beyond knowing.

How can the rivers and lakes of a surging and swelling world
hinder your journey? For sage wisdom, trust boat and carriage.

81

Dark-Enigma-Sands Traveled

When Dark-Enigma-Sands Mountain traveled to the district of Sedge-Field, he was welcomed with a hundred celebrations. The next day, he asked the venerable abbot Meager-Pool Mountain: "All that hullabaloo yesterday, where's it gone now?"

Meager-Pool lifted up the bottom corner of his robes.

"That has nothing to do with a wren startling away," said Dark-Enigma-Sands.

GATHA

Boat hidden in the valley of night
and oar revealed in crystal springs,
dragon and fish never contemplating water, their natural place:

every fiber of their being broken, they incite primal-unity itself,
Dark-Enigma-Sands and Meager-Pool, together like

box and cover, arrow shaft and tip,
flagpole and sky, shadow and grass.

Recluses, they're ancient turtles nesting among lotus blossoms,[109]
rainbow fish drifting celebration, frolicking amid water-grasses.[110]

82

Cloud-Gate Sound Color

Instructing the assembled sangha, Cloud-Gate Mountain said: "To hear a sound is itself Way awakened. And to see a color is itself mind enlightened. Avalokitesvara, the World-Gaze Bodhisattva, once went to buy a gruel-cake. He put his money down, only to discover he'd bought an elegant steamed bun."[III]

GATHA

Leap-Stallion chased out the gate, his rebellion swept away,[112]
smoke and dust of ten thousand kingdoms clears on its own.

The twelve fields of perception free of sight and sound, idle,
enlightenment sets this three-thousand-realm Cosmos ablaze.

83

Way-I Visiting Doctor

River-Act Mountain asked Way-I Mountain: "Where have you been?"

"I went to visit the doctor," replied Way-I.

"Are many people sick?"

"Some people are sick," explained Way-I, "and some are healthy."

"You're one of those who is healthy, aren't you?"

"Healthy or sick: that has nothing to do with anything. Speak! Speak!"

"And what does talk have to do with anything?"

GATHA

Even spirit-lightning doctors can't fathom his pulse,
so how could wondrous medicine ever pass his lips?

If he continues alive in this world, he'll remain at root Absence,
and if he dies back into emptiness, he'll remain at root Presence:

never extinguished—and so, ever living;
never perishing—and so, life perennial.

Ancestor back beyond those most primordial Buddhas,
he wanders alone after the final empty kalpa, become

himself the vast tranquility this sky shelters and earth supports,
wheeling around with turning sun soaring and moon rushing on.

84

Million-Million One Finger

Whenever a question was posed, Master Million-Million simply raised one finger.

GATHA

Old Master Million-Million wielded his exquisite fingertip Ch'an,
wielded it on and on across thirty long years and never used it up:

it's a method truly beyond schemes other masters of Way concoct.
He looks, and finds nothing anywhere mundane or commonplace,

and the sheer clarity of that realization
keeps teaching and practice wide-open.

You can drink this thousand Buddha-sea Cosmos in the least fact,
but people expect boundless dragons to alight in their open hands:

they bow in homage to teachers who share out their gigantic catch.
Meanwhile, sage Million-Million simply raises a finger and shouts:

Look! Look!

85

Prajna-Devotion Shrine-Tower

Emperor Source-Ancestral Awe asked Nation-Teacher Prajna-Devotion: "Your hundred-year life is ending. Afterward, what can I do for you?"

"Build this old monk a shrine-tower stitched from Absence," replied Prajna-Devotion.

"What style of shrine-tower?" asked the emperor.

Prajna-Devotion was silent for some time, then said: "You don't understand."

"No, I don't."

"I've entrusted the dharma to a monk named Source Tiger-Glare. He knows all about these things."

After Prajna-Devotion's death, the emperor summoned Source Tiger-Glare and asked him to explain. Source said:

South of Appearance River, north of Deep-Lake River:
there at the center, you'll find enough gold for the whole country.

Beneath a tree casting Absence-shadow, accord-whole boats drift:
it's the crystalline hall of meditation. You recognize no one there.

GATHA

Looking round and round alone,
perfect as a Buddha-truth pearl
and lofty as ranged peaks, the eye's precision exacts this world:

moon setting in deep lakes of emptiness, night's color doubled;
cloud revealing scattered scraps of autumn's mountain splendor.

Positions of the eight trigrams rectified,[113]
ch'i-force of the five elements balanced:
when you're there in your own original place, what do you see?

Prajna-Devotion and Tiger-Glare—O—
                           they only appear to understand such things,
and India's Buddhas and patriarchs—O—
                           they never fathomed existence-tissue itself.

86

Dark-Enigma Great Awakening

When he was a student, Purport Dark-Enigma asked Yellow-Bitterroot Mountain: "What is the Buddhadharma's vast *ch'i*-deep insight?"

Yellow-Bitterroot struck Dark-Enigma a blow. After this had happened three times, Dark-Enigma left Yellow-Bitterroot and traveled to see Dolt-Vast. Dolt-Vast asked: "Where have you come from?"

"From Yellow-Bitterroot," replied Dark-Enigma.

"How did Yellow-Bitterroot teach you?"

"Three times I asked about the Buddhadharma's great *ch'i*-deep insight, and three times I was struck. I don't know if I was at fault or not."

"Yellow-Bitterroot's such a kind old grandmother! He cleared away your troubles just like that. And you come asking if you're at fault!?"

Hearing these words, Purport Dark-Enigma had a great awakening.[114]

GATHA

Fledgling capable of anything at all,
colt ready to run thousands of miles,

flute singing in thusness-clarity wind,
wordless loom-of-origins at the very

hinge of things—he's wild lightning-flight splitting the original-face,
magisterial sun soaring alone where confusions of cloud break apart.

Tug at a tiger's whiskers,[115]
gaze into Absence itself,
and you're just like Dark-Enigma: a great sage-elder, noble and valiant.

Scatter Mountain Presence Absence

When he was a traveling monk, Scatter Mountain went to see River-Act Mountain and asked: "I hear, Master, that you often say: *All that talk of Presence, talk of Absence: it's like a vine growing on a tree. If the tree suddenly comes crashing down, where has that vine's ravaged talk gone?*"

River-Act Mountain roared with glorious laughter.

"I bought meditation-cushions and came four thousand miles," complained Scatter. "Why are you playing games with me?"

River-Act asked an attendant to get some money and repay the distinguished monk. Then he made a prediction: "One day, a lone-eye dragon[116] will break it all open for you."

Later, Scatter Mountain journeyed to see Lumen-Illumine and told him what had happened. Lumen said: "Old River-Act was head to tail right there at the very hinge of things, head to tail. But he wasn't facing someone who understood his mind that deeply."

Scatter Mountain pressed on: "But when the tree comes crashing down, where has that vine's ravaged talk gone?"

"It's gone to make River-Act start laughing again."

Hearing this, Scatter was awakened, and thereupon cried out: "River-Act Mountain's laughter came roaring out of origins, and it was bristling with fangs."

GATHA

Vine ravaged on crashed tree asking River-Act Mountain, glorious
laughter roaring a strange idleness: it took that bristling-with-fangs[117]

laughter to break such probing open. When words and ideas cease
being the path, you enter deep inside that loom-of-origins gateway.[118]

88

Hewn-Beam Not Seeing

The *Hewn-Beam Sutra* says: "When I'm not seeing original-nature,[119] why don't you look at the place I am when I'm not seeing original-nature? If you see that terrain clearly, you'll see occurrence-appearing-of-itself is nothing other than the very form of that not-seeing. If you don't see clearly, occurrence-appearing-of-itself seems to be something else. But how could it not be you yourself?"

GATHA

In this vast ocean of things gone bone-dry,
this limitless Cosmos of emptiness brimful,

a patchrobe monk's original-face endures on and on,
the tongues of ancient Buddhas fallen utterly silent.

Strung-Pearls stars twisting through nine meanders,
jade-pure loom-of-origins barely begun its weaving,

we meet in such absolute clarity there's no one at all to recognize.
That's when you begin to see you have no companions anywhere.

89

Fathom Mountain No Grass

Instructing the assembled sangha, Fathom Mountain said: "This is the end of our summer session. Autumn's beginning, my friends, and you're all leaving. Wherever you travel, east or west, you must go to that place where there's no wild-grass for ten thousand miles, not a single inch."

Then he continued: "Existence-tissue itself: it alone stretches for ten thousand miles without an inch of wild-grass. So, how do you get there?"

When a monk traveling from that summer session told Stone-Frost Mountain about this, Stone-Frost said: "Step out the gate, and already there's wild-grass everywhere."

A century later, Solar-Vast Mountain said: "To tell the truth: don't step out the gate, and it's still a flood of wild-grass stretching far and wide."

GATHA

Wild-grass floods far and wide
inside the gate, outside the gate: just look into your own nature.

They say it's easier to wander thorn-bramble thickets than find
realization in that moonlit night out beyond the meditation hall,

but look! Look!
There are so many ways you

dwell like a huge and ancient tree, all wizened and bitter cold
and about to follow spring wind on into depths of blazing scar.

90

Reliance Mountain Sounds Mallet

Master Reliance Mountain had a dream in which he traveled across future kalpas to the assembly of Maitreya Buddha, where he was given the second seat. Soon, one of the Buddhas there sounded the announcement mallet and pronounced: "Today, our second seat elucidates dharma."

Reliance Mountain rose, sounded the mallet himself, and said: "Mahayana dharma is outside the four existential distinctions and free of their hundred negations.[120]

"Pay exacting attention to this right here," he concluded, as he sounded the announcement mallet again: *crack!* . . . *crack!*

GATHA

In his dream, disguised as a patchrobe monk amid that assembly of elders,
he sat in the seat of honor among venerable sages arrayed in lavish ranks,

open-hearted mind-ground yielding nothing. That announcement mallet's
crack! . . . crack!: it was Buddha's lion-roar elucidating dharma fearlessly,

mind tranquil as boundless seas,
courage vast as Northern Dipper,

ocean-dragon eyes weeping tears,
oyster heart open, pearl revealed.[121]

Who can see how rambling yammer disdains our loom-of-origins nature?
Dragon-shaggy eyes full of laughter, he passed on wordless transmission,

done with clever ideas like *existential distinctions and negations,*
done treating disease caused by medicine, like Way-Entire's clan.[122]

91

Wellspring-South Peony Blooming

High Minister Solar-Extent Continual said to Wellspring-South Mountain: "Dharma-Master Sangha-Fundament[123] was absolutely wondrous. He explained so clearly: *This heaven-and-earth Cosmos everywhere shares the same root, and the ten thousand things everywhere share the same original potency.*"[124]

Pointing to a peony blooming in the courtyard, Wellspring said to Solar-Extent: "This is your very life, but you see this peony as if it were some kind of dream-mirage."

GATHA

Illuminating Absence and Presence, you fathom Changemaker roots,[125]
and wandering this confusion of appearance and disappearance, you

find the gate.[126] Letting spirit drift beyond kalpas frees you of questions,
and gazing deep into things at hand, understanding abides in mystery:

tiger roars and desolate winds howling and howling among cliffwalls,
dragon cries over and over, fathom-deep cloud shading into darkness.

The way people live in dream: Wellspring-South broke it wide-open,
and that, that alone makes him magisterial as those Buddhas to come.

92

Cloud-Gate Perfect Jewel

Grand-Master Cloud-Gate Mountain said: "Within all heaven and earth, this seed-time breath-space home,[127] the perfect jewel lies hidden right here at the center, in this mountain of ten thousand forms that is the mind. To reveal it, take a dragon-weave lantern into the Buddha Hall, then toss those three gates of liberation[128] into the flame."

GATHA

Bundle away what thoughts remain, and give up shiny pursuits,
then you're out on these far shores of life. Where is home here?

After centuries away, Master Wood-Cutter found no road home,
and Lord Jar-Gourd always had his gourd house hanging nearby,

but here, the night moon floats across this river's golden waves,
and blooming silver-grass leans together in wind-blown autumn

snow flurries. Cold fish up from depths ignore the bait and drift.
Crystalline song rises, falls—and your turning raft wanders free.

93

Yokel-Patriarch Not Understanding

Yokel-Patriarch Mountain asked his dharma-brother Wellspring-South Mountain: "That Buddha-truth pearl people don't recognize: they say that we must find it within ourselves, and also that it's hidden in the Buddha Existence-Tissue Arrival womb. So, what is that womb?"

"It's you and this old teacher coming and going, living this life," replied Wellspring.

"And our stillness—no coming and no going?"

"That too is the womb."

"Then what is the pearl?" asked Patriarch.

Wellspring called out: "Master Patriarch!"

Patriarch nodded in assent.

Wellspring shouted: "Get out! You're not understanding anything I say!"

GATHA

Far from *yes this* and *no that*, radiance gain and loss share,
it's what minds always mirror, what hands always point at.

Coming and going, no coming and going: either
way, this life is itself that existence-tissue womb.

Ruler of the great wheeling Cosmos bestows its realization,
primordial emperors realized it in Absence perfectly empty:

it's the loom-of-origin's turning pivot, the great teacher. You
patchrobe monks, eyes enlightened clarity: don't rush blindly through life!

94

Fathom Mountain Was Unwell

Fathom Mountain was unwell. A monk asked: "You are ill, Master, but aren't there plenty of folks here who aren't ill?"

"There are."

"Can't they help you heal?" continued the monk.

"First I need to heal all that insight they're clinging to," declared Fathom.

"And once you do that, Master, what happens?" asked the monk.

"Then they see there's no illness."

GATHA

Forget about this stinking skin-bag of a body,
chuck this red lump of heart: that leaves your

original-face right here at the hinge of things,
original-mind right now all *yang*-deep heaven.[129]

Old doctor seeing there is no primordial ailment we inherit:
that young monk tried to heal him and couldn't come close,

but it's easy: when autumn rains end, wildland streams thin;
where summer clouds vanish, ancient mountains grow cold.

So why invent problems,
why keep pissing around?

Done with transformation and realization, he was so utterly
enlightened, so utterly awake in his solitude—just like you!

95

Dark-Enigma Draws Horizon

Purport Dark-Enigma asked the vice-abbot: "Where have you been?"

"I was at the city market, selling our yellow millet," replied the vice-abbot.

"Did you sell it all?"

"Every bit."

Dark-Enigma scratched a single line in the dirt with his travel-staff, then said: "And what about that primal-unity line, horizon line that first separated heaven and earth[130]—did you sell that, too?"

"KHO-AAA!" shouted the vice-abbot.

Dark-Enigma struck him a blow.

Later, Dark-Enigma told the head-cook what had happened, and the head-cook said: "The vice-abbot didn't understand your *ch'i*-deep meaning, Master."

"And you?" said Dark-Enigma. "What would you have done?"

The head-cook bowed reverently. Dark-Enigma struck him a blow.

GATHA

Dark-Enigma exhausted the loom-of-origins. Lofty in wild nobility,
he looked clear into things, parsed them to an autumn hair's-breadth,

and sweeping crafty foxes and rabbits away, whirled up precipitous
Ch'an winds and lightning strikes translating fish into sage dragons.[131]

Life-bringing sword,
death-dealing blade—
he could slice through radiant cloud and sky, split a windblown hair.

Supreme teacher, he complicated the flavor of things into such depths,
and there where we feel everything at once, who are you facing it all?

Nine-Peak Didn't Approve

When he was young, Nine-Peak Mountain served as Stone-Frost Mountain's attendant. After Stone-Frost returned to the great transformation of things, the sangha wanted to ask the head-monk to succeed him as abbot. Nine-Peak didn't approve, and said: "Wait. Let me question him first. If he understands our former teacher's *ch'i*-deep insight, I'll gladly serve him as I did our former teacher." Then he asked the head-monk: "Our former teacher said *Set out in silence. Set out in stillness. Set out in a single ten-thousand-year primal-unity thought. Set out in cold ash and skeletal trees. Set out in simple robes of sun-bleached silk.* What aspect of this grand and wondrous affair was he illuminating?"

"He was illuminating the grand and wondrous things of this world as a single tissue," replied the head-monk.

"I see," declared Nine-Peak. "You don't understand our former teacher's *ch'i*-deep insight at all."

"You don't approve?" challenged the head-monk. "Then bring me some incense."

He lit the incense, and said: "If I don't understand our former teacher's *ch'i*-deep insight, I won't be able to set out in liberation before this incense burns down."

After saying this, he sat on his meditation-cushion and soon liberated himself from this world.

Putting his hand on the head-monk's shoulder to comfort him, Nine-Peak said: "You can liberate yourself into death while sitting, like some sage-masters of old; or amid the bustle of daily business, like others. But either way, even a glimpse of our former teacher's *ch'i*-deep insight is beyond even your wildest dreams."

GATHA

Stone-Frost transmitted our source-ancestral
essence to old Nine-Peak. And that guy who

set out in liberation, incense burning, never
knew this blood-pulse at the hinge of things.

Moon-nest crane amid thousand-year dreams, he sat in a snowy house
deluded, no idea the grand and wondrous things of this world are one

tissue. End meditation, and the ten distances of time and space remain,
exquisite. Take one silent step in, and you see the dragon wild in flight.

97

Radiant-Alike Regal Hat

Emperor Radiant-Alike confided to Burgeon-Change: "Dead center at the source, I secured the singular Buddha-nature jewel. But now there's no one who can estimate its value."

"Hand me the jewel, and I'll take a look," offered Burgeon-Change.

The emperor grabbed the edge of his regal hat with both hands and pulled it down tight over his head.

"That jewel of yours," declared Burgeon-Change, "who could even begin to estimate its value?"

GATHA

That emperor shared *ch'i*-deep insight with someone kindred enough,
and all beneath heaven turned toward him, minds sincere as sunflowers.

His invaluable Buddha-nature jewel found at the dead-center source,
utterly beyond precious jade and gold in legends of ancient kingdoms,

that source-depth Buddha-nature jewel revealed to Burgeon-Change:
it's such singular radiance and illumination. Who could name a price?

Radiant-Alike's treasure is itself teacher to ten thousand generations,
luminous dharma-gold wheel dazzling all beneath these four heavens.

98

Fathom Mountain Cutting Clean

A monk asked Fathom Mountain: "Of the Buddha's three esoteric bodies, which is not numbered among the endless variety of things and ideas?"

"I'm constantly cutting clean through to the intimate essence of this," replied Fathom.

GATHA

Not tangled in the world's affairs,
not clinging to deep origin-tissue:
that empty jar of karma is itself Ch'an's wordless transmission.

Silver duckweed, gossamer wind: evening on the autumn river.
Ancient shoreline, boat returning home: a single ribbon of mist.

99

Cloud-Gate Bowl Pail

A monk asked Cloud-Gate Mountain: "What is the entrance every fleck of dust offers into three-shadowed-earth *samadhi*?"

Cloud-Gate replied: "Rice in the rice-bowl, water in the water-pail."

GATHA

Rice in the rice-bowl, water in the water-pail:
speaking his fearless heart, he hoped to find one who understood.

Pause to ponder: you lose the loom-of-origins, the six patriarchs,
and suddenly, meeting face to face means ten million miles apart.

But Cloud-Gate tried to bring students close.
Insight offering intimacy tight as sliced gold—O—
                             sliced gold, is there anyone kindred enough?
You need the vagabond mind of a rebel stone—O—
                             rebel stone, it alone is capable of such things.

100

Jewel-Fang Rivers Mountains

A monk asked Master Jewel-Fang Awake: "It was all Buddha's crystalline source-tissue clarity in the beginning. But how could it suddenly give birth to rivers and mountains and this vast earth?"

"It was all Buddha's crystalline source-tissue clarity in the beginning," said Awake. "But how could it suddenly give birth to rivers and mountains and this vast earth?"

GATHA

To see Presence and not Presence: it's like
turning your hand palm-down and palm-up.

That guy wandering about Jewel-Fang Mountain
keeps right up with Wary-Cloud Buddha himself![132]

Notes

NAMES WORK VERY DIFFERENTLY in ancient China. We almost never think about the meaning of names. But in ancient China, it was all about meaning. Artist-intellectuals adopted names for their meanings, choosing meanings that they felt somehow expressed their essential artistic or philosophical natures. Ch'an monks and teachers followed this rule in especially dramatic ways, giving themselves "dharma-names" or adopting names of local mountains (which were themselves given meaningful names). As translation of ancient Chinese texts involves most fundamentally translating a culture, it follows that those names should be rendered not simply in their romanized form, but according to their meanings: the Sixth Patriarch's name, Hui Neng, therefore becomes Prajna-Able, for example, and Yün Men becomes Cloud-Gate Mountain.

Chapter titles take the form of four-word set-phrases. A set-phrase is a telegraphic four-word phrase that refers somehow to an ancient text or legend, distilling into four scarcely grammatical words all the dimensions of a story or anecdote or idea. The Chinese often use such set-phrases in writing and speech to make a complex point in an elegant and terse way, and there are so many set-phrases that they are collected in special dictionaries.

1. For a full discussion of Ch'an meditation, see the two "Meditation" chapters in my *China Root*, pp. 27–34 and 103–12.
2. For a full explanation of how sangha-cases functioned in Ch'an practice, see the "Sangha-Case" chapter in my *China Root*, pp. 113–19.
3. **ch'i:** see Key Terms, p. 219.
4. See *The Way of Ch'an* for Kuo Hsiang (p. 62f.) and these passages (p. 65), which are from his very influential commentary on the *Chuang Tzu*.
5. **The World-Honored-One:** Shakyamuni Buddha.
6. **Manjusri:** A mythological bodhisattva described as teacher to the Seven Buddhas of mythic antiquity who lived in successive kalpas (world-cycles each lasting 4,300,000 years), one per kalpa, the most recent of whom was Shakyamuni

Buddha. Manjusri is also described as embodying the wisdom of all Buddhas. In Sanskrit, Manjusri means "Gentle Glory," but as one might expect in Ch'an, the Chinese transliteration (文殊) means something like "Sutra-Kill."

7. **inner-pattern:** see Key Terms, p. 219.

8. **loom-of-origins:** see Key Terms, p. 220.

9. War-True was a very pious Buddhist in the conventional sense of sutra study and gaining merit through donations to Buddhist institutions.

10. **Absence:** see Key Terms, p. 217.

11. **Star River:** our Milky Way.

12. **origin-tissue:** see Key Terms, p. 218.

13. **existence-tissue:** see Key Terms, p. 218.

14. **Cold Mountain . . . Fathom-Gather:** Cold Mountain was the legendary outsider Ch'an poet (for whom see my *The Way of Ch'an,* pp. 187ff.), who wrote of following a scrap of road high into his wild mountain home, and Fathom-Gather (Shih Te) was his sidekick.

15. Although seemingly a mythic tale from ancient India, this story interestingly reflects native Ch'an understanding. The most common ideogram for *monastery* or *temple* is 寺, which portrays a hand below (showing wrist with fingers and thumb) touching a seedling above (showing stem and branches growing up from the ground). This seedling image means "earth" as the generative source, so the graph's full etymological meaning becomes something like: "touching the generative." And so, Ch'an practice as an attentive cultivation of or attention to the generative nature of things—a point developed in the accompanying *gatha.*

16. **faintly-emergent smile:** This is the same phrase used for Mahakasyapa's smile at seeing Buddha holding up a flower. In this mythic tale of Ch'an's first dharma transmission, the smile is evidence for Mahakasyapa's enlightenment. See entry for *shadowed emergence* in Key Terms (p. 220) and *The Way of Ch'an* (p. 14).

17. **goddesses Prosperity and Destitution:** A legend tells of goddess Prosperity coming to visit a home bringing good fortune. But the householder soon learns that Prosperity always travels with her sister, Destitution.

18. *ch'i*-**weave insight:** see Key Terms, pp. 225–26.

19. Wisdom-Hoard and Hundred-Elder were dharma-brothers who had received dharma transmission together from Patriarch Sudden-Horse Way-Entire.

20. **sutras . . . shastras:** In Indian Buddhism, sutras were considered the words of Buddha himself, and shastras were commentaries on those sutras or treatises on Buddhist doctrine and practice.

21. **Emperor Cobra:** In mythic times, the earth was unshaped and flooded. The sage-emperor Cobra (Yü) cut channels for rivers, raised mountains, and otherwise shaped earth's terrain to make it habitable.

22. **Lady She-Voice:** In Chinese mythology, Lady She-Voice (Nü Kua) was the wife of the first emperor. They were half human and half dragon. At that time, the Cosmos was out of whack. The sky didn't cover the earth, and earth

didn't wholly support the sky. The four directions were askew. Fire burned everywhere, and water cascaded everywhere. Lady She-Voice smelted stone and patched it all together.

23. **Gate:** Recuring often in *The Carefree-Ease Record* and throughout the Ch'an tradition, *gate* refers to the courtyard gate through which one enters a monastery (or any traditional Chinese dwelling). Its complementary and more explicitly philosophical meaning is "an entrance-way to insight." And so, to pass through the gate is to attain enlightenment. See also Introduction, pp. xi–xii.

24. **three realms:** In conventional Buddhism, this is traditionally given as the desire realm, the form realm, and the formless realm—three strata of reality into which sentient beings are reborn after death depending on their karma. In Ch'an, it would mean something like Absence, Presence, and the generative force driving the process of change, as Absence generates the ten thousand things of Presence in perpetual transformation.

25. **perfect dharma of the eye's treasure-house:** When Buddha held up the flower and Mahakasyapa smiled, revealing his understanding, Buddha described (in Chinese texts) that understanding "not relying on words and texts, outside teaching and beyond doctrine" as "my perfect dharma of the eye's treasure-house." As such, this idea continued through the Ch'an tradition as the essence of insight and awakening.

26. **KHO-AAA!:** This shout was Purport Dark-Enigma's signature way of revealing/teaching Ch'an's deepest insight. Hence, Purport Dark-Enigma is saying that students must find their own way, not simply master the teacher's insight.

27. For the original version of this sangha-case in Purport Dark-Enigma's teaching record, see my *The Way of Ch'an*, pp. 218–19.

28. In one of Ch'an's most famous stories, the Sixth Patriarch was an illiterate peasant who outwitted the admired head-monk. He was given the dharma-robe of transmission in the middle of the night, then fled to avoid the enmity of jealous monks.

29. **transmitting the lamp:** In Ch'an Buddhism, this lamp is absolute insight, which is passed from teacher to student directly, outside of word and text, idea and institution. Hence: transmission of the lamp. One of the major texts in Ch'an literature is the *Lamp-Transmission Record*, which recounts enlightening stories from Ch'an's lineage of great teachers.

30. **Two-Moon bird:** From the opening sections of *Chuang Tzu*, the first of which is:

> In Northern Darkness there lives a fish called Bright-Posterity. This Bright-Posterity is so huge that it stretches who knows how many thousand miles. When it changes into a bird, it's called Two-Moon. This Two-Moon has a back spreading who knows how many thousand miles, and when it thunders up into flight its wings are like clouds hung clear across the sky. It churns up the sea and sets out on its migration to Southern Darkness, which is the Lake of Heaven.

31. **jaws jutting out:** Anyone whose jaws were visible from behind was popularly thought to be malicious and untrustworthy.

32. **South Mountain:** Calling up such passages as "like the timelessness of South Mountain" in the ancient *Book of Songs*, poets often called local mountains "South Mountain" to suggest a kind of mythic stature as an embodiment of the elemental and timeless nature of the earth.

33. **idleness:** see Key Terms, p. 223.

34. *yes this* **and** *no that*: This phrase/idea is a motif in the *Chuang Tzu*, where it describes judgment/choice as a prime example of conceptualization that alienates consciousness from the generative movement of Way.

35. **distinction:** see my *China Root* (p. 61) for the philosophical dimensions of this recurring Ch'an concept and its role in awakening.

36. Here, Dharma-Eye is referring to a passage from the "Fact-Mind Inscription" (*The Way of Ch'an*, p. 140):

> A hair-width distinction is error
> enough to split heaven and earth:
>
> to face Tao's shimmering Way,
> simply give up like and dislike,
>
> for battling things you dislike
> is mind's great disease. It hides
>
> wordless dark-enigma depths,
> turns tranquil thought into toil.

37. **has:** This word, which also occurs in the preceding question, is 有 (Presence). 有 pairs with Absence, which appears below, to describe the foundational cosmological/ontological framework of Taoism/Ch'an. Like 無, it has a productive double meaning: "is/has" + "Presence." See Key Terms, p. 216.

38. **no ... Absence:** These are the same word repeated: 無, which is often used in Taoist and Ch'an texts for its rich double meaning: "no" + "Absence." See "Key Terms" entries for *Absence* (p. 217) and *Absence-action* (p. 222).

39. A pared-down version of this sangha-case appears as the first sangha-case in *No-Gate Gateway*. See my translation, pp. xxiii–xxvi (discussion) and pp. 4–6 (sangha-case and commentary). In that version, altogether different in import, it became the most preeminent of sangha-cases. For the original version of this encounter in Visitation-Land's teaching record, see my *The Way of Ch'an*, p. 226. And cf. p. 227 for a variation.

40. **Sumeru Mountain:** Mythic mountain that rises out of a vast sea and stands at the center of the Buddhist universe as its axis point.

41. **gateway:** The term *gateway* (關) refers first to gateways in mountain passes at the frontier, which can be either locked to block passage or opened to allow passage. And so, the idea that it is a gateway one must open and pass through into realization. As such, it figures prominently throughout the Ch'an

tradition, most notably in the third of the classic sangha-case collections, *No-Gate Gateway*.

42. Master Snow-Peak Mountain suggested that enlightenment was like charming a viper without getting bit. For the entire story, see my *The Blue-Cliff Record*, Case 22.

43. **gossamer . . . dark female-enigma Way:** Borrowed from the *Tao Te Ching*, seminal text of Taoism, chapter 6:

> The valley spirit never dies.
>
> It's called *dark female-enigma*,
> and the gateway of dark female-enigma
> is called *the root of heaven and earth*,
>
> gossamer so unceasing it seems real.
> Use it: it's effortless.

44. **travel-staff:** Rough-hewn walking-stick, perhaps seven feet tall, which is cut in the mountains and left mostly in its natural state. Carried by monks as they traveled the country visiting Ch'an monasteries to learn from different masters, the travel-staff came to symbolize essential Ch'an insight, original Buddha-nature, etc.

45. **Rhino*x*eros:** *Rhinoceros* is 犀牛: literally, *rhinoceros* + *ox*. Both ideograms contain the graph for ox: 牛. Interestingly, this is what Prosper-Sustain Mountain chooses to write in the origin-mind circle rather than the single graph for *rhinoceros*.

46. **origin-mind circle:** Widely known by its later Japanese name, *enzo*, an origin-mind circle is the image of emptiness drawn with *wu-wei* spontaneity. Hence, it is a distillation of enlightenment's most basic and essential nature.

47. The system of Buddhist institutions had grown huge, accumulating vast and tax-exempt wealth. It was crippling the nation, so in 845 the government dismantled it, destroying many monasteries and sending monks back to more practically productive endeavors.

48. **seal:** People's names were engraved into the end of elongated precious stones ("chops"), which were then used to stamp identification seals on documents, books, art works, etc. The same word (印) is used both for the seal and the engraved stone used to imprint that seal. This doubling makes a perfect image for Ch'an's direct mind-to-mind transmission.

49. **Buddha-truth pearl:** In a kind of Ch'an mythology, a black-dragon coils around the Buddha-truth pearl clutched in its claws, and heroically raiding the dragon's watery lair and seizing that pearl is the goal of Ch'an practice, tantamount to enlightenment. This dragon clutching the pearl in its claws is the subject of many powerful paintings. For the dragon, see Key Terms, p. 221.

50. **kalpa:** A world-cycle of 4,300,000 years.

51. **Star River:** Our Milky Way.

52. **Origin-Dark:** see Key Terms, *Origin-dark quiet*, p. 220.

53. **golden-scale fish:** see the *gatha* below and its note.

54. **. . . Three-Cascade Gorge . . . :** Gorge where the mythic Emperor Cobra sliced a passage for the Yellow River through mountains. Ascending the waters cascading through this gorge is a Ch'an figure for the practice leading to enlightenment, and that enlightenment is likened to a golden-scale fish struck by lightning and transformed into a sage dragon that soars away through the sky.

55. **red-fin adrift . . . :** An echo of Chuang Tzu's contented fish moving with "carefree-ease." See Introduction, p. ix.

56 **pearl:** see note 49.

57. For the original version of this sangha-case in Purport Dark-Enigma's teaching record, see my *The Way of Ch'an*, p. 213.

58. For the original version of this sangha-case in Visitation-Land's teaching record, see my *The Way of Ch'an*, p. 230.

59. **Indra's jewels . . . net:** Indra is the god of sky and divine guardian of the dharma. Surrounding his palace is a boundless net of jewels, each of which reflects all the other jewels and also all the reflections in all those jewels. An image for the complete interpenetration of all things, especially the sangha of all sentient beings, and a profound vision of the Cosmos as a tissue of mutual interrelation, even mutual identity. This has recently been adopted by deep ecologists as an image for earth's interwoven ecosystem.

60. **guest . . . host:** "Host" (主) has two specialized Ch'an meanings: first, "host" as a master or teacher, and opposed to "guest" (客) as a student who would enter the monastery as a guest; and second, "host" as one's original Buddha-nature, or empty-mind, and "guest" as one's everyday-mind with its thoughts and memories. These two meanings are parallel, as empty-mind is finally the teacher, and for a student, everyday-mind is trying to learn from empty-mind.

61. **"Confronting Grief" . . . Flood-Gauze River:** Ch'ü Yüan (ca. 340–278 B.C.E.) is the earliest identifiable poet in Chinese literary history. After writing "Confronting Grief," a long poem of political lament (see my *Classical Chinese Poetry: An Anthology*, pp. 69–71), he threw himself into Flood-Gauze River and drowned.

62. **seed-time breath-space:** 宇宙, which is generally translated "space and time." But that imposes a whole Western metaphysical scheme on the Chinese worldview. In fact, both ideograms contain the image for a roof at the top. Below that, 宇 has the image for breath spreading in the space beneath the roof, hence: "breath-space home," and 宙 has the image for a seed sprouting beneath the roof, hence: "seed-time home." All of this makes sense, of course, in the Taoist/Ch'an framework wherein reality is seen as a nurturing home and an organic and ever-emergent process of transformation. Hence the translation used here: *seed-time breath-space home.*

63. **Sumeru Mountain:** see note 40.

64. According to cultural legend, the invention of writing in mythic times was inspired by bird tracks and bark-beetle tracings.

65. **fish frolic:** Another echo of Chuang Tzu's *carefree-ease* fish. See Introduction, pp. ixff.

66. For the original version of this sangha-case in Visitation-Land's teaching record, see my *The Way of Ch'an*, p. 224. And cf. p. 225 for a variation.

67. **nonduality:** Existence-tissue reality seen as an undifferentiated whole, with no difference between: Absence and Presence, delusion and awakening, subjective and objective (and in the terminology of conventional Buddhism: *samsara* and nirvana). And because words and thoughts create these distinctions, it is empty-mind that makes this nondual perspective possible.

68. **Vimalakirti:** The scene described here is the setting of the *Vimalakirti Sutra*. Vimalakirti suffers a sickness that comes from his deep sympathy for the suffering of this world, and indeed his name in Chinese means something like "touch-allied." Sage Vimalakirti was known for his fundamental critique of Buddhist teachings by asserting radical nonduality: that there is no basis for the oppositions essential to Buddhist teaching: *samsara* and nirvana, delusion and awakening, etc

    Manjusri: see note 6.

69. **dharma-realm expanses:** The physical universe in all its thusness.

70. **portrait:** Crucially, this term (真) means both "portrait" (here) and "wild thusness all clarity-absolute" (below).

71. This conversation refers to Fathom Mountain's famous enlightenment story:

    When he was about to leave Cloud-Crag Mountain, Fathom Mountain asked: "A hundred years from now, if someone asks me about your most utter *ch'i*-weave insight, how shall I answer simply?"

    Cloud-Crag was silent for a long time. Then, he said: "Simply this! This right here!"

    . . .

    Fathom was adrift in doubt. But later, wading across a stream, he caught sight of his reflection in the water and had a great awakening to Cloud-Crag's wordless *ch'i*-weave insight.

72. **fifth watch:** There were five watches in the night, two hours each, beginning at 7 p.m. and ending at 5 a.m. Hence, the fifth watch was between 3 a.m. and 5 a.m.

73. **ch'in:** Ancient stringed instrument much revered by Chinese intellectuals as a means for attaining enlightenment, the *ch'in* often appears in poems and was used as accompaniment when Chinese poets chanted their poems. In the hands of a master, a *ch'in* could voice with profound clarity the rivers-and-mountains realm, empty-mind, even the very source of all things.

74. **trigrams and knotted cords:** Proto-linguistic forms of notation: knotted cords are known to us from pre-Columbian Americas as *quipu*, and trigrams are the eight three-line elements that are paired in every possible combination to form the sixty-four hexagrams of the *I Ching* (see my *I Ching: The Book of Change*).

75. **Swirl-Roam:** Old Swirl-Roam (盤古: P'an Ku) was a primordial human-like creature who evolved from primal chaos. When he died, his body became the Cosmos.

76. **Changemaker:** Personification of the generative power of the existence-tissue: Tao or *tzu-jan*.

77. **Great Potter's wheel:** The Great Potter was another personification of the generative power of the existence-tissue: Tao or *tzu-jan*. Interestingly, the term "Great Potter's wheel" (甄陶) also refers to Yellow-Bitterroot's skillful teaching methods.

78. **Prosperity and Destitution goddess:** see note 17.

79. **southland sudden-awakening sage:** Referring to Sixth Patriarch Prajna-Able, who founded the southern school of Ch'an that advocated instantaneous enlightenment, as opposed to gradual enlightenment that comes through a process of learning from teachers who "cackle at" students.

80. **axe-handle:** Wisdom-Expanse pushes the idea of self-reliant demolition to its limit here: not engaging with teachers, smashing the game of Ch'an itself, and finally even breaking the instrument of that smashing. But "axe-handle" has a further resonance here as the model used in sage instruction (reaching back to its first appearance in *The Book of Songs* #140), because when you use an axe to shape a new axe-handle, "the pattern's close at hand."

81. **smash . . . oven open:** A village shrine had a sacred oven where people sacrificed many creatures. One day, unhappy about all those animals dying, an abbot went to that village and rapped on the oven with his staff. The oven thereupon broke into pieces and a god emerged who said he had been cursed by karmic retribution and thanked the abbot for liberating him. The abbot came to be known as Oven-Smasher.

82. **seclusion-fast:** periods of seclusion during which monks intensified practice and ate especially simple meals.

83. **single line . . . :** The ideogram for the number one is a single horizontal line (一), and it carries a kind of mythic status in the minds of ancient Chinese. Its deepest philosophical meaning is "primal-unity." And further: it is the first gesture, the initial act of differentiation imposed on undifferentiated reality (primal-unity). As such, it inscribes the horizon line that first separated heaven and earth.

84. **Sumeru Mountain:** see note 40.

85. **Sakradevanam Indra:** Supreme deity of Vedic mythology, a sky god who lives on a peak in Thirty-Three-Peak Heaven. He rules the weather in particular (cf. carp and rain in the following sentence), with the help of the thirty-two devas who live on the other thirty-two peaks.

86. **peels eyelids away:** Enlightenment is sometimes described as eyelids peeled away, leaving awakened sight wide-open.

87. **fish-traps and rabbit-snares:** Reference to a famous passage from the *Chuang Tzu* (26.8):

The point of a fish-trap is the fish: once you've got the fish, you can forget the trap. The point of a rabbit-snare is the rabbit: once you've got the rabbit, you can forget the snare. And the point of a word is the idea: once you've got the idea, you can forget the word.

How can I find someone who's forgotten words, so we can have a few words together?

88. Dharma-Eye studied for a long time under Reward-Perpetua Mountain without attaining enlightenment. Eventually he went on a pilgrimage to visit other teachers. Caught in a snowstorm, he sheltered at Earth-Hoard Mountain's monastery. There, he was awakened after the encounter with Earth-Hoard Mountain that is retold in Case 20.

89. **Lumen-Abyss:** The seminal poet T'ao Ch'ien (365–427 C.E.), also known as T'ao Yüan-ming: Tao "Lumen-Abyss." Lumen-Abyss spoke of these overgrown paths in his famous "Back Home Again Chant," a poem about returning to recluse life on his farm, for which see my *The Selected Poems of T'ao Ch'ien*, p. 33. For T'ao Ch'ien and his role in the birth of Ch'an, see my *The Way of Ch'an*, pp. 75ff. and 107ff.

90. **occurrence-appearing-of-itself:** see Key Terms, p. 222.

91. **Buddha Existence-Tissue Arrival:** see Glossary of Buddhist Terms, p. 231.

92. **dharma-realm:** The physical universe in all its thusness.

93. **eyelids pinched closed:** Enlightenment is sometimes described as eyelids peeled away, leaving awakened sight wide-open.

94. These three figures were dharma brothers of Kingfisher-Cliff Mountain, all historically important teachers who reappear in *The Carefree-Ease Record* and are probably commenting when they heard this story at their own far-flung monasteries.

95. **hexagrams:** The six-line diagrams of the *I Ching*, which were considered the most primordial form of written language.

96. **Absence dwelling:** In another example of the philosophically productive double meaning of 無, this phrase is also be read "non-dwelling" (a reading extended at the beginning of the *gatha*).

97. *yang*-**deep heaven . . .** *yin*-**deep earth:** Heaven and earth were considered the grandest manifestations of the cosmological principles *yang* and *yin*. See Key Terms, p. 221.

98. **Samantabhadra Buddha:** Primordial Buddha and embodiment of the original purity of all phenomena in both this everyday realm of *samsara* and the peaceful realm of nirvana.

99. **Maitreya Buddha:** The Buddha to come, whose appearance during the next kalpa will issue in an earthly paradise.

100. **birth and death:** Not seriously in the sense of conventional Buddhism's karmic system, but in the Ch'an sense: as the "source-tissue root" from which the ten thousand things are born and into which they die, Absence is "perennial,"

without birth or death. So, to be free of birth and death is to realize one's truest nature as integral to this Absence-tissue.

101. **Buddha-truth pearl . . . dragon den:** see note 49.

102. **great jewel:** Recurring metaphor for the sage who has realized original nature, and emphasizing the idea that we are in our original nature always, already awakened.

103. **third watch:** The nighttime hours between 11 p.m. and 1 a.m. For more, see note 72.

104. **origin-mind circle:** see note 46.

105. For the original version of this encounter in Cloud-Gate Mountain's teaching record, see my *The Way of Ch'an*, p. 240.

106. **dharma-talk flagpole:** A flag was raised on the monastery flagpole to indicate that a dharma-talk is imminent. Hence, an image for enlightened talk and ideas, which are not to be trusted.

107. **Shadowed-Emergence:** see Key Terms, p. 220.

108. **Star River raft:** After flowing out to sea in the east, the Yangtze and Yellow Rivers were thought to ascend and rarify, becoming the Star River (Milky Way). This celestial river then crosses the sky and descends in the far west to form the headwaters of the Yangtze and Yellow Rivers. The legend of the Star River raft tells of a Yangtze fisherman who one day saw a strange raft floating past his house. It was empty, so he climbed aboard, wondering where it might take him. The raft carried him downstream and eventually up into the Star River, where it became a star known as the Wandering Star and slowly drifted back across the sky toward the west.

109. **lotus blossoms:** Because its exquisite beauty is rooted in mud and murky water, the lotus flower in conventional Buddhism is the image of pure Buddha-mind untainted by the world of compromise and struggle in which we live our everyday lives.

110. **rainbow fish . . . :** Another echo of Chuang Tzu's *carefree-ease* fish. See Introduction, pp. ixff.

111. It's interesting to compare Cloud-Gate Mountain's use of gruel-cake here and in Case 78.

112. **Leap-Stallion:** Infamous rebel whose defeat ended social chaos and reestablished the relatively stable Han Dynasty.

113. **trigrams:** The eight three-line elements that are paired in every possible combination to form the sixty-four hexagrams of the *I Ching*, representing every possible "position" in the great transformation of things. See my *I Ching: The Book of Change*.

114. For the original version of this encounter in Purport Dark-Enigma's teaching record, see my *The Way of Ch'an*, pp. 211–12. That original is much longer and more complicated, and comparison reveals how dramatically Wisdom-Expanse often distilled traditional Ch'an tales to emphasize their essences.

115. **Tug at a tiger's whiskers:** In the original version of this tale, Purport Dark-Enigma returns to Yellow-Bitterroot Mountain after his awakening and challenges him forcefully. Yellow-Bitterroot howls: "You crazy maniac! You come back here and tug at this tiger's whiskers!?"

116. **dragon:** see Key Terms, p. 221.

117. **idleness:** see Key Terms, p. 223.

118. **gateway:** see note 41.

119. **seeing original-nature:** The definition of awakening in the seminal Bodhi-dharma poem (p. 229) and throughout the tradition.

120. **four existential . . . negations:** A complicated system of ontological/metaphysical speculation from ancient Indian philosophy and logic.

121. **pearl:** see note 49.

122. This line echoes Case 6, both sangha-case and *gatha*.

123. **Sangha-Fundament:** Seng Chao (374–414), early scholar-monk who was instrumental in amalgamating Ch'an from native Taoism and imported Buddhism. See my *The Way of Ch'an*, pp. 78ff.

124. **potency:** see Key Terms, p. 220.

125. **Changemaker:** Personification of Tao or *tzu-jan*, the generative force driving change.

126. **gate:** see note 23.

127. **seed-time breath-space home:** see note 62.

128. **three gates of liberation:** The main gate of a monastery (traditionally having three separate doors). Or alternately, the three practices that lead to liberation, which are variously identified. For the *gate* in Ch'an, see note 23.

129. *yang*-**deep Heaven:** see note 97.

130. **primal-unity line . . . :** see note 83.

131. **translating fish into sage dragons:** see note 54.

132. **Wary-Cloud:** Chinese transliteration for the Sanskrit *Gautama*.

Key Terms

AN OUTLINE OF CH'AN'S CONCEPTUAL WORLD

CH'AN'S CONCEPTUAL WORLD is described fully in my *China Root: Taoism, Ch'an, and Original Zen*. That book serves as the full philosophical introduction to this one. But Ch'an's conceptual world is easily outlined by defining a few foundational terms/concepts that recur often in the Ch'an literature. In fact, these concepts are inevitably crucial when Ch'an touches philosophical ground—but they have been misconstrued, mistranslated, and often simply untranslated: a process that has largely erased original Ch'an from modern Zen.

Our understanding of Ch'an/Zen changes dramatically when we realize that these terms all come from early Taoist philosophy. By probing deeper into the native understanding of key terms/concepts, a new Ch'an is revealed. It is a Ch'an grounded in the rich earth of Taoist cosmology/ontology, reality experienced as a generative tissue—a Ch'an for which spiritual practice aspires to reintegrate consciousness with that tissue in perpetual transformation. Concepts at this foundational level blur, and Taoist terminology proliferates. So, what we find here in a survey of Ch'an's key terms is a host of concepts, often nearly synonymous, each offering a different way into the fundamental nature of consciousness and Cosmos.

This Key Terms section functions as a glossary to those terms/concepts, and it is also designed to be read straight through as an introductory essay describing Ch'an's conceptual framework—which means, unfortunately, it cannot follow alphabetical order. Here is an alphabetical index to the terms:

Absence, 217
Absence-action, 222
Actualization, 220
Awakening/Enlightenment, 228
Ch'i, 219
Ch'i-deep insight, 225
Ch'i-weave mind, 225
Dark-enigma, 218
Dragon, 221
Emptiness, 224
Empty-mind, 227
Existence-tissue, 218
Eye/Sight, 228
Heaven and earth, 221
Idleness, 223
Inner-pattern, 219
Loom-of-origins, 220
Mind, 225
Mirror, 228
No-mind, 227
Occurrence-appearing-of-itself, 222
Origin-dark quiet, 220
Potency, 220
Presence, 216
Shadow-emergent/Shadowed-emergence, 220
Source-ancestral, 223
Thusness/Thusness all clarity-absolute, 219
Unborn/Absence-born, 224
Way (Tao), 217

PRESENCE 有

The empirical universe, described in Taoist philosophy as the ten thousand things in their perennial transformations.

ABSENCE 無

The generative source-tissue from which the ever-changing realm of Presence perpetually arises. This undifferentiated tissue is the ontological substrate infused mysteriously with a generative energy. We might almost describe it in scientific terms as matter itself: the formless material that is shaped into the ten thousand discrete forms of reality (Presence) and into which those forms dissolve at death. Because of its generative nature, it continuously shapes itself into the individual forms of the Cosmos, then reshapes itself into other forms: the ten thousand things in the constant process of change. So, a more literal translation of Absence might be "without form," in contrast to "within form" for Presence. Absence is known directly in meditation, where it is experienced as empty consciousness itself, known in Ch'an terminology as "empty-mind" or "no-mind" (see p. 227): the formless generative source of both thoughts and the ten thousand things. Hence, meditation as a spiritual practice reintegrating consciousness and Cosmos.

WAY (TAO) 道

The Tao of Taoism. *Tao* originally meant "way," as in pathway or roadway, a meaning it has kept. But Lao Tzu reconceived it as a generative cosmological process, an ontological "path*Way*" by which things come into existence, evolve through their lives, and then go out of existence, only to be transformed and reemerge in new forms. As such, it might provisionally be divided into Presence and Absence. Here is a prime example of overlapping terminology struggling to name the fundamental nature of reality, for in practice Way / Tao emphasizes the undifferentiated and generative nature of the existence-tissue, and is therefore nearly synonymous with Absence. Indeed, Lao Tzu describes it as "source" and "female" and "mother."

Tao represents one of the most dramatic indications that Ch'an is a refinement and extension of Taoism, because the term *Tao* is used extensively in Ch'an with the same meaning. It sometimes simply means "Ch'an's *way* of practice, its path*Way* to enlightenment," a usage that parallels its early use in Taoism and Confucianism. But more often, and more philosophically important, it is the Taoist Way / Tao, that generative ontological source-tissue. And sometimes it is both simultaneously, as in the quintessential Ch'an dictum: "Ordinary mind is Way."

DARK-ENIGMA 玄

Perhaps the most foundational concept in this Taoist-Ch'an cosmology/ontology, *dark-enigma* is Way before it is named, before Absence and Presence give birth to one another—that region beyond name and ideation where consciousness and the empirical Cosmos share their source. *Dark-enigma* came to have a particular historic significance, for it became the name of a neo-Taoist school of philosophy in the third and fourth centuries C.E.: Dark-Enigma Learning (see my *The Way of Ch'an*, p. 47ff.), a school that gave Chinese thought a decidedly ontological turn and became central to the synthesis of Taoism and *dhyana* Buddhism into Ch'an. And indeed, the concept is at the very heart of Ch'an practice and enlightenment. It is there at the very beginning, concluding the first chapter of the *Tao Te Ching*: "dark-enigma deep within dark-enigma, / gateway of all mystery." And it recurs often at key moments throughout the Ch'an tradition. Among the countless examples is Fathom Mountain (Tung Shan) saying that the most profound dimension of Ch'an's wordless teaching is dark-enigma within dark-enigma, which he evocatively describes as the "tongue of a corpse." And the very influential Stone-Head (Shih T'ou) ends his still-influential poem "Amalgam-Alike Compact" declaring dark-enigma to be the essential object of Ch'an inquiry:

> Please, you who try to fathom dark-enigma clear
> through, don't pass your days and nights in vain.

ORIGIN-TISSUE 緣
EXISTENCE-TISSUE 如

緣 and 如 are virtually synonymous with Absence, Tao/Way, and dark-enigma: reality as a single tissue, undifferentiated and generative. Birth, giving form to the ten thousand individual things, is described as 緣合: "origin-tissue coming together." And death, the unraveling of individuation, is described as 緣離: "origin-tissue scattering." So the vast and ongoing transformation of things is this *origin-tissue* coalescing into individual forms and then dispersing back into a single undifferentiated tissue. And it is important for Ch'an that this tissue is the "thusness" we encounter every moment in our everyday life, as emphasized in the recurring phrase 真如: "wild existence-tissue thusness," or "existence-tissue all thusness-clarity absolute.

THUSNESS / THUSNESS ALL
CLARITY-ABSOLUTE, ETC. 真

The sheer presence of reality in and of itself, free of our ideas and stories: reality experienced as sheer wonder and mystery. There is no end of Ch'an stories revealing this thusness as the whole of Ch'an, as the most profound of teachers, especially in its most magisterial form as rivers-and-mountains landscape. As such, it returns consciousness to empty-mind or mirror-mind (see pp. 227–28), wherein its "clarity-absolute" becomes the very content of consciousness or identity: a major dimension of awakening.

CH'I 氣

氣 is often described as the universal life-force breathing through things. But this presumes a dualism that separates reality into matter and a breath-force (spirit) that infuses it with life. Like the Absence/Presence dichotomy, that dualism may be useful as an approach to understanding; but more fully understood, *ch'i* is both breath-force and matter simultaneously. It is a single tissue generative through and through, the matter and energy of the Cosmos seen together as a single breath-force surging through its perpetual transformations. And so, *ch'i* is nearly synonymous with Way and Absence, but emphasizing their generative dynamism.

INNER-PATTERN 理

The philosophical meaning of *inner-pattern*, which originally referred to the veins and markings in a precious piece of jade, is something akin to what we call natural law. It is the system of principles or patterns that governs the unfolding of *Way* (or Absence, or *ch'i*) into the various forms of the ten thousand things in their perennial transformations. It is a pervasive concept in the Ch'an tradition, where moving integral to inner-pattern is one definition of awakening.

POTENCY 體
ACTUALIZATION 用

Together, these terms represent an important pair of foundational cosmological/ontological concepts in Chinese philosophy. *Potency* refers to the inherent potentiality or nature of things: a virtual synonym for *inner-pattern*. That "potency" gives shape to the particular "actualization," the ongoing emergence (expression/manifestation) of things in the world.

ORIGIN-DARK QUIET 幽
SHADOW-EMERGENT/
SHADOWED-EMERGENCE 微

Appearing often in Ch'an recluse poetry, 幽 always infuses its surface meaning "quiet solitude" with rich philosophical depths, beginning with the sense of "dark/secret/hidden/mystery." That leads finally to the term's deepest level, "origin-dark quiet," the level where it forms a terminological pair with 微. Here it means forms, the ten thousand things, just on the not-yet-emergent side of the origin-moment: just as they are about to emerge from the formless ground of Absence, or just after they vanish back into that ground. The everyday meaning of 微 is "faint/sparse/hidden," but in poetic and philosophic contexts, it takes on cosmological/ontological dimensions: things on the emergent side of the origin-moment in that cosmology of Tao's ongoing generative unfolding, just barely coming into existence as differentiated entities or not quite vanished back into the undifferentiated ground.

LOOM-OF-ORIGINS 機

A mythological description of Way's unfurling process. Hence, the Cosmos in its perennial transformation seen as an ever-generative loom-of-origins. Chuang Tzu, the seminal Taoist sage, describes it like this:

"The ten thousand things all emerge from a loom-of-origins, and they all vanish back into it."

DRAGON 龍

Another mythical incarnation of Way and its ten thousand things tumbling through their traceless transformations, dragon was feared and revered as the awesome force of change, as the embodiment of all creation and all destruction. Its form was therefore in constant transformation. To take one example: small as a silkworm and vast as all heaven and earth, dragon descends into deep waters in autumn, where it hibernates until spring, when its reawakening means the return of life to earth. It rises and ascends into sky, where it billows into thunderclouds and falls as spring's life-bringing rains. Its claws flash as lightning in those thunderclouds, and its rippling scales glisten in the bark of rain-soaked pines.

HEAVEN AND EARTH 天地

Heaven has a number of intertwined meanings that often function simultaneously. Originally a kind of impersonal divinity, the seminal Taoist sages reinvented *heaven* as an entirely empirical phenomena—the generative cosmological force that drives the ongoing transformation of natural process—thereby secularizing the sacred while at the same time investing the secular with sacred dimensions. This transition moment was soon superseded by the entirely secular *Way* (*Tao*), which was essentially synonymous with *heaven*, but without the metaphysical implications.

Heaven appears often in the phrase "heaven and earth," meaning the world of our everyday experience, for 天 means most simply "sky." But the phrase also means "the universe" in Taoism's cosmological sense, for *heaven and earth* were conceived as the grandest cosmological manifestations of *yang* and *yin*. Hence, the universe conceived as a living and dynamic interpenetration of *yang* and *yin*.

From this comes a second set of terms for heaven and earth: 乾 and 坤. These terms, the titles of the first two hexagrams of the *I Ching*, emphasize heaven as *yang* (the active generative force of the Cosmos) and earth as *yin* (the receptive generative force): the two forces whose ceaseless interaction generates the process of change. Accordingly, 乾 and 坤 might be read as "Creative" and "Receptive," or more descriptively: "*Yang*-Deep Heaven" and "*Yin*-Deep Earth."

OCCURRENCE-APPEARING-OF-ITSELF   自然

A central concept in early Taoist cosmology/ontology, 自然 (*tzu-jan*) is a name for the process of Way that emphasizes individual entities rather than the process as a whole. Its literal meaning is "self-so" or "the of-itself," which, as a philosophical concept, becomes "being such of itself," hence "spontaneous" or "natural." But a more revealing translation of *tzu-jan* is "occurrence-appearing-of-itself," for the term is meant to describe the ten thousand things burgeoning forth spontaneously from the generative source (Presence from Absence), each according to its own nature, independent and self-sufficient, each dying and returning to the process of change, only to reappear in another self-generating form. As such, this inheritance from Taoism continued as a major element in Ch'an's conceptual framework.

ABSENCE-ACTION   無為

If there is a single term that describes the nature of sangha-case practice (see Introduction, p. xvi) and Ch'an enlightenment, it is 無為 (*wu-wei*). Like *tzu-jan*, *wu-wei* dates to the earliest levels of Taoist thought and means literally "no/Absence (*wu*)" + "acting (*wei*)." A spiritual practice broadly adopted by ancient artist-intellectuals, it became central to Ch'an practice—further indication of Ch'an's essentially Taoist nature. *Wu-wei* means "not acting" in the sense of acting without the metaphysics of self, or of being *absent* when you act. This selfless action is the movement of *tzu-jan*, so *wu-wei* means acting as an integral part of *tzu-jan*'s spontaneous burgeoning forth out of Absence into Presence.

Wu-wei is perhaps the original exploitation of the double meaning of 無 (no/Absence) that became crucial in Ch'an. Examples include *unborn/Absence-born* and *no-mind/Absence-mind* (for which, see pp. 224, 227), and a host of other variations: no/Absence knowing, no/Absence thought, no/Absence form, no/Absence dwelling, no/Absence dharma, no/Absence practice, no/Absence enlightenment. This double meaning opens to the deepest level of *wu-wei*'s philosophical complex, where the term's alternate sense of "Absence" + "acting" means *wu-wei* action is action directly from, or indeed *as*, the ontological source. We see in sangha-cases Ch'an masters dramatizing this in their wild antics (behavior that likens them to Chuang Tzu's zany Taoist sages): to practice *wu-wei* is to move with the wild energy of the Cosmos itself. But it also takes the form of unbridled mental processes: indeed, the *Lamp-Transmission Record* says "*wu-wei* is meditation." Taken altogether, *wu-wei* represents a return to Paleolithic consciousness. And it is, again, the very definition of Ch'an enlightenment, enlightenment that is ideally the form of everyday life.

SOURCE-ANCESTRAL 宗

In the blur of concepts at deep cosmological/ontological levels, *source-ancestral* seems virtually indistinguishable from Way or Absence or inner-pattern, and it is at times described as equivalent to Absence-action (*wu-wei*). The full dimensions of this concept are revealed dramatically in the etymologies of its two pictographic elements: 宀 and 示. 宀 simply means "roof," and is a stylized version of ∩, the early form that portrays a side-view of the traditional Chinese roof with its prominent ridgeline and curved form. 示 derives from 川 and the more ancient oracle-bone form 𝍤, showing heaven as the line above, with three streams of light emanating earthward from the three types of heavenly bodies: sun, moon, and stars. These three sources of light were considered bright distillations of or embryonic origins of *ch'i*, the breath-force that pulses through the Cosmos as both matter and energy simultaneously. Hence, 宗 is the cosmological source of *ch'i* as a dwelling-place, a dwelling-place that is the very source of the Cosmos.

The common meaning of 示 was simply "altar," suggesting a spiritual space in which one can be in the presence of those celestial *ch'i*-sources. And indeed, enlightenment in Ch'an was to inhabit this dwelling-place altar, as it was for Chuang Tzu, who described a sage as one who "holds fast to the source-ancestral." And indeed, the common meaning of 宗 is "ancestor," which suggests a remarkable sense of the source as ancestral to us, as kindred. And so, the source-ancestral as always already our very nature.

IDLENESS 閑, 閒

Way unfurls its process of transformation in an effortless and spontaneous movement that can be described as idleness. Recognizing this,
ancient China's artist-intellectuals and Ch'an adepts took living in idleness as a spiritual ideal, a kind of meditative wandering in which you
move with the improvisational movement of Absence-action. And so, it
is Absence-action enacted in the context of everyday life.

Etymologically, the character for idleness connotes "profound serenity and quietness," its pictographic elements rendering a tree standing
alone within the gates to a courtyard: 閑, combining two pictographic
elements more clearly visible in their early forms as 門 (gate: showing
double doors) and 木 (tree: showing a trunk with branches above and
roots below). Or in its alternate form, a moon shining through open
gates: 閒, which replaces 木 with) (moon).

UNBORN/ABSENCE-BORN 無生

無生 plays on the two meanings of 無 in much the same way as 無為
(*wu-wei*), to give: "no/Absence (*wu*) + born/alive (*sheng*)." 無生 means
"not living" in the sense of living with the metaphysics of self *absent*,
hence: "selfless living." This opens to a deeper level in which the term
means "Absence-born" or "Absence-alive," describing our most essential
identity as Absence itself. And finally, 無生 also means "not born" or
"unborn," describing the fact that we are each a fleeting form conjured
in Tao's process of perpetual transformation: not just born out of it and
returned to it in death, a familiar concept that still assumes a center of
identity detached from the Cosmos and its processes, but never *out of it*,
totally unborn. Indeed, our fullest identity, being unborn, is Way itself,
is therefore all and none of earth's fleeting forms simultaneously. And so,
the double meaning is beautifully complementary, for to be "unborn" is
precisely to be "Absence-born/alive. This unborn dwelling is the goal of
sangha-case practice.

EMPTINESS 空, 虛

In its native Taoist and Dark-Enigma Learning context, *emptiness* is essentially synonymous with *Absence*: emptiness in the sense of undifferentiated reality *empty* of individual forms, reality as a single formless and generative tissue to which we belong. It was used to (mis-)translate the Sanskrit *sunyata* (for which, see "Glossary of Buddhist Terms," p. 233), a crucial moment in the creation of Ch'an. Free of the metaphysical dimensions of *sunyata*, 空 and 虛 are entirely this-worldly, notably in their common meaning "sky," archetypal form of emptiness in our everyday experience. Etymologically, the two elements of 空 portray *labor* (工, early form: 㠯 suggesting something emerging from an absence, and labor is of course to make something where there was nothing) within a *cave* (穴, indicating the space beneath a roof 宀, stylized version of ∩, side-view of the traditional Chinese roof with its prominent ridgeline). Hence, a generative emptiness in earth, a womb where the work of gestation happens. 虛 in its early forms contains a pair of mountainpeaks (⌒) and, in the space above those peaks, the element for *tiger* (虎, deriving from early images like 㐬). Together, these two elements form 虛, literally: "mountain tiger-sky." This emphasizes the sense of emptiness as sky/heaven: however, rather than emptiness as mere stillness (as in conventional Buddhism), it is emptiness dynamic with the wild energy of a tiger. And so, the two complementary terms (which often appear together in Ch'an texts) suggest at their origins something like emptiness in its heavenly and earthly forms, and *heaven and earth* is a Chinese term for the Cosmos itself.

MIND 心
CH'I-WEAVE MIND/CH'I-DEEP INSIGHT 意

In Ch'an parlance, *mind* principally refers to consciousness emptied of all contents, a state revealed through deep meditation: hence, mind as "original-nature" or "Buddha-nature." This consciousness in its original-nature is nothing other than Absence, that generative cosmological tissue—for it is the empty source of thought and memory, and also an empty mirror open via perception to the ten thousand things of

Presence. So, once again: Ch'an's conceptual world as fundamentally Taoist in nature.

Ch'an sometimes also uses *mind* seemingly in the common English sense of the word, as the center of language and thought and memory, the mental apparatus of identity. It seems the same, but Taoist-Ch'an cosmology/ontology makes it radically different. Those processes of mind were described as 意, which has a range of meanings: "intentionality," "desire," "meaning," "insight," "thought," "intelligence," "mind" (the faculty of thought). The natural Western assumption would be that these meanings refer exclusively to human consciousness, but 意 is also often used philosophically in describing the nonhuman world, as the "intentionality/desire/intelligence" that shapes the ongoing cosmological process of change and transformation (here it is virtually synonymous with *inner-pattern*). Each particular thing, at its very origin, has its own 意, as does the Cosmos as a whole. 意 can therefore be described as the "intentionality/intelligence/desire" infusing Absence (or Tao) and shaping its burgeoning forth into Presence, the ten thousand things of this Cosmos. It could also be described as the "intentionality," the inherent ordering capacity, shaping the creative force of *ch'i*.

This range of meaning links human intention/thought to the originary movements of the Cosmos—for it operates in a cosmological context recognizing an "intelligence" that infuses all existence, and of which human thought is but one manifestation. So, 意 is a capacity that human thought and emotion share with wild landscape and, indeed, the entire Cosmos, a reflection of the Chinese assumption that the human and non-human form a single tissue that "thinks" and "wants." Hence, thought/identity is not a transcendental spirit-realm separate from and looking out on reality, as we assume in the West. Instead, it is woven wholly into the ever-generative *ch'i*-tissue, into a living "intelligent" Cosmos— and so, it seems best translated as *ch'i*-weave mind, *ch'i*-weave/deep insight, *ch'i*-weave thought, etc.

This concept appears perhaps most famously in the perennial Ch'an question: "What is the *ch'i*-weave mind Bodhidharma brought from the West?" This is said to be asking about the essence of Ch'an. Normal translations such as "purpose" or "meaning" cannot support such a claim—but once 意 is understood as "*ch'i*-weave mind," that claim makes sense, because then it's asking about mind woven into the generative tissue of the Cosmos. This is the heart of Ch'an understanding and enlightenment, and indeed one basis for the claim that we are always already enlightened.

EMPTY-MIND   空心, 虛心
NO-MIND   無心

The understanding of mind outlined above is the context within which we must understand one goal of Ch'an practice: to see through *mind* as the analytical faculty to *mind* as consciousness emptied of all contents. From this come the terms *empty-mind* or *no-mind*—which are, confusingly, virtually synonymous with *mind* in its primary Ch'an sense. And they are central to Ch'an awakening, but awakening as more than the simple emptiness and tranquility of conventional Buddhism as it arrived in China.

For empty-mind was recognized as Absence itself, that generative cosmological/ontological tissue, source in consciousness of thought, memory, emotion, etc. And so, empty-mind was now dynamic and alive, an understanding emphasized in the etymological dimensions of 虛: "mountain tiger-sky," a poetic description of dynamic emptiness if there ever was one. And rather than an ascetic pursuit for a mind of tranquility and stillness, a state that is always forced and temporary (illusory!), Ch'an's Taoist assumptions allow an embrace of emptiness as the generative tissue of Absence, Tao, Cosmos. Hence, an acceptance of ordinary mind as always already awakened, always already Buddha, Tao, *tzu-jan*, *wu-wei*.

It is the same for *no-mind*. Because of the ever-productive double meaning of 無 (no/Absence), 無心 (no-mind) describes mind both empty of content and made of the generative source-tissue (Absence-mind). It is accordingly here often translated "Absence no-mind." And so, again, an embrace of mind's processes as already awakened.

In ancient China, there was no fundamental distinction between heart and mind: 心 connotes all that we think of in the two concepts together. In fact, the ideogram is a stylized version of the earlier 心, which is an image of the heart muscle, with its chambers at the locus of veins and arteries. This integration of mental and emotional realms means the experience of empty- or no/Absence-mind cultivated in Ch'an practice is not just a spiritual or intellectual experience, but also a rich emotional experience.

EYE/SIGHT 目, 眼, 見, 直, ETC.
MIRROR 鏡, 鑑

Once mind is emptied of all content (through meditation and sangha-case practice), the act of perception becomes a spiritual act: Absence no-mind mirror-deep, empty-mind mirroring the world, leaving its ten thousand things free of all thought and explanation—utterly simple, utterly themselves, and utterly sufficient. This image of the mirror is foundational in Taoism and Ch'an, recurring at key moments throughout the tradition. And it is the heart of Ch'an as a landscape practice. In such mirror-deep perception, earth's vast rivers-and-mountains landscape replaces thought and even identity itself, revealing the unity of consciousness/identity and landscape/Cosmos that is the heart of sage dwelling not only for Ch'an practitioners, but for all artist-intellectuals in ancient China. Indeed, when Buddha held up the flower and Mahakasyapa smiled, the understanding he revealed was exactly that: the mirror-deep seeing of empty-mind. And in the Ch'an tradition, Buddha describes that understanding "not relying on words and texts, outside teaching and beyond doctrine" as "my perfect dharma of the eye's treasure-house." This idea continued through the tradition as the essence of insight and awakening, for it encapsulates another way of meeting Buddha and all the patriarchs directly, but also of being indistinguishable from them, of being Buddha oneself.

AWAKENING/ENLIGHTENMENT 悟 / 見性

In Chinese, these two terms may seem quite different at the outset—but in the end, they describe the same awakening/enlightenment. 悟 (Japanese: *satori*) is composed etymologically of *mind* (心 appearing here in stylized form as 忄 on the left) and *me* (吾) on the right. This renders the term's common meaning of "waking" from sleep as a suddenly renewed awareness of "my mind," or perhaps "me" returning to "mind" again. And that becomes in the Ch'an context something very close to a "sudden awakening" (that essential Ch'an principle) to empty-mind as "original-nature." 見性 (Japanese: *kensho*) means "see + original-nature," where the ideogram for "original-nature" is composed of *mind* again on the left and *birth* on the right, hence "mind at its origin." This realization, an observational clarity almost scientific in nature, becomes the definition of enlightenment in the last line of Bodhidharma's seminal poem:

A separate transmission outside all teaching
and nowhere founded in eloquent scriptures,

it's simple: pointing directly at mind. There,
seeing original-nature, you become Buddha.

In spite of their apparent differences, the two terms both describe enlightenment as an awakening to oneself, to one's inherent or original-nature—and because that original-nature is whole and silent, prior to our mental machinery of words and concepts, awakening is instantaneous and outside of teaching and practice. That original-nature is unborn and empty, is in fact Way or Absence itself. And so, awakening/enlightenment is, again, a selfless "wandering boundless and free" through the selfless transformations of Way's vast and ongoing process.

For a full account of Ch'an awakening/enlightenment, see the Awakening chapter in my *China Root* (pp. 126–36).

Glossary of Buddhist Terms

BUDDHA　佛

Buddha refers most literally to Shakyamuni/Gautama, the historical Buddha, and also to a host of other Buddhas in Buddhist mythology. Beyond its use as an element of storytelling, Ch'an invests no faith in that mythology. And Ch'an is primarily interested in Shakyamuni at the deep level of his essential nature, which is his empty-mind. So the meaning of the term *Buddha* expands to mean empty-mind, emphasized in the term *Buddha-nature*; and because empty-mind is the central concern of Ch'an, Buddha also came to mean the essence of Ch'an. Indeed, Ch'an's cultivation of empty-mind opens the possibility both of meeting the Buddha and the patriarchs directly, but also of being indistinguishable from them, of being Buddha oneself. And finally, as empty-mind is indistinguishable from Absence or dark-enigma, Buddha becomes synonymous with those terms too, and even the generative Way (Tao) itself. Hence, *Buddha* is absorbed into the Taoist cosmology, becoming another term used to describe that generative tissue that remains always just beyond language. Further, the ideogram for Buddha is made up of the elements for "person" and "loom (-of-origins)." And from here, *Buddha* logically comes to mean reality itself—a usage we often find in the Ch'an tradition, and which has the effect of infusing our everyday world with a sense of the sacred. In particular, Buddha is identified with rivers-and-mountains landscape.

BUDDHA EXISTENCE-TISSUE ARRIVAL　如來

Tathagata is a name for Buddha describing his nature as the "thus-come" or "thus perfected one." In its original Indian context, this would suggest an enlightened sage who has entered nirvana. In the Chinese transliteration, it means "existence-tissue arrival." Hence, Buddha has been transformed into a virtual equivalent of Way (Tao) or Absence— the generative "existence-tissue" (see Key Terms, p. 218) that is always, in its ongoing process of transformation, a moment of "arrival." Or alternately, as an enlightened sage who has "arrived" by inhabiting his original-nature as integral to the "existence-tissue."

DHARMA 法

Dharma in Ch'an can refer to the teachings of the Ch'an tradition. But Ch'an's essential teaching is outside of words and ideas, and here is *dharma*'s most fundamental meaning: the sheer thusness of things that is the true teaching. And this is actually the term's primary use in Ch'an— virtually synonymous with *tzu-jan*, *Tao*, *Absence* (*emptiness*), *dark-enigma*, even *Buddha*. Another example of a Buddhist term being adapted to function at the deepest cosmological/ontological levels of the Taoist conceptual world.

PRAJNA 慧, 般若

In Indian Buddhism, *prajna* refers to a transcendental state of perfect wisdom in which one directly sees or even becomes the fundamental emptiness (*sunyata*: see below) of things. Reconceived in the entirely empirical terms of Taoist cosmology/ontology, it is defined in a host of related ways in the Ch'an tradition, but a good working definition is mind returned to its original-nature as "Absence," which is equated with empty-mind as a "dark-enigma mirror." This reveals a profound shift from Sanskrit/Buddhism to Chinese/Ch'an, for *prajna* has been recon-figured into a Taoist concept. Again, metaphysics replaced by the great transformation itself: this wild earth we inhabit.

SAMADHI 三昧地

In the *dhyana* Buddhism that migrated to China from India, *samadhi* simply meant "consciousness emptied of all subjective content," the goal of meditative practice. But its Chinese transliteration means "three-shadowed earth." And so, *dhyana*'s abstract and cerebral meditative state has been invested with the earthly dimensions of Taoism / Ch'an: empty-mind free of all conceptual structures, self dismantled completely by the Ch'an wrecking-crew, leaving consciousness open to its "original-nature" as the Cosmos moving in perfect tranquility at that all-encompassing and perennial origin-place that Lao Tzu called *Absence*. In its consummate description of enlightenment, *No-Gate Gateway* declares that in awakening "you wander the playfulness of *samadhi*'s three-shadowed earth."

SAMSARA   輪迴

Samsara's traditional Buddhist meaning is "the illusory universe we inhabit as we work out our karmic destiny," a meaning sometimes referenced derisively in Ch'an. Generally though, *samsara* refers in Ch'an to the phenomenal universe of our everyday experience.

SUNYATA   空, 虛

In its original Indian Buddhist context, *sunyata* means "emptiness"—but "emptiness" in the sense that things have no intrinsic nature or self-existence, that they are illusory or delusions conjured by the mind. Here, it is closely associated with *nirvana* as a state of selfless and transcendental extinction or *emptiness*. This *sunyata* emptiness is essentially metaphysical, suggesting some kind of "ultimate reality" behind or beyond the physical world we inhabit. But this atmosphere of metaphysics is quite foreign to the Chinese sensibility and Ch'an. Indeed, there was no word in Chinese with the meaning of *sunyata*. 空 and 虛 (*emptiness*: see Key Terms, p. 224), with their superficial similarities, were quite simply the only possibility. In the Taoist context, *emptiness* is virtually synonymous with *Absence*, reality seen as a single formless and generative tissue that is the source of all things—a concept altogether different from the Buddhist *sunyata*. Translation and interpretation of Ch'an in modern America often treat 空 and 虛 as *sunyata*—but in the Chinese, the term has lost its Sanskrit meaning, replacing it with the native Chinese one. Indeed, this reinvention of *sunyata* as 空 and 虛 was a defining moment in the creation of Ch'an.

Index to Ch'an Teachers

1. English Names with Chinese Equivalents

English	Wade-Giles	Pinyin	Sangha-Case
Azure-Forest Mountain	Ch'ing Lin	Qing Lin	59
Bodhidharma	P'u-T'i Ta-Mo	Pu-Ti Da-Mo	2
Bull's-Eye Altar	Chung Yi	Zhong Yi	72
Burgeon-Change	Hsing Hua	Xing Hua	97
Cloud-Crag Mountain	Yün Yen	Yun Yan	21, 49, 54
Cloud-Gate Mountain	Yün Men	Yun Men	11, 19, 21, 24, 26, 31, 40, 61, 71, 78, 82, 92, 99
Crag-Summit Mountain	Yen T'ou	Yan Tou	22, 43, 50, 55, 75
Crag-Talisman Mountain	Jui Yen	Rui Yan	75
Dark-Enigma-Sands Mountain	Hsüan Sha	Xuan Sha	21, 24, 81
Dharma-Eye	Fa Yen	Fa Yan	17, 20, 27, 51, 64, 74
Dice-Thrown Mountain	T'ou Tzu	Tou Zi	63
Dragon-Fang Mountain	Lung Ya	Long Ya	80
Earth-Hoard Mountain	Ti Tsang	Di Zang	12, 20, 64
Far-Waters Mountain	Lo P'u	Luo Pu	35, 41
Fathom Mountain	Tung Shan	Dong Shan	22, 49, 56, 80, 89, 94, 98
First Mountain	Shou Shan	Shou Shan	65, 76
Flax-Canyon Mountain	Ma Ku	Ma Gu	16
Gauze Mountain	Lo Shan	Luo Shan	43

ENGLISH	WADE-GILES	PINYIN	SANGHA-CASE
Heart-Sight Mountain	Te Shan (Hsüan Chien)	De Shan (Xuan Jian)	14, 22, 52
Heaven-Peak Mountain	Ch'ien Feng	Qian Feng	40, 61
Hundred-Elder Mountain	Po (Pai) Chang	Bai Zhang	6, 8
Iron-Grinder	T'ieh Mo	Tie Mo	60
Jewel-Fang Awake	Lang-ya Chiao	Lang-ya Jiao	100
Kingfisher-Cliff Mountain	Ts'ui Yen	Cui Yan	71
Kingfisher Shadowed-Emergence	Ts'ui Wei	Cui Wei	80
Lumen-Whole	Te Shan (Yüan Ming)	De Shan (Yuan Ming)	46
Manifest-Revere	Chang Ching	Zhang Jing	16
Medicine Mountain	Yao Shan	Yao Shan	7
Million-Million	Chu Ti	Zhu Di	84
Mirror-Sight Mountain	Te Shan	De Shan	55
Mongrol-Grain	Mi Hu	Mi Hu	62
Nine-Peak Mountain	Chiu Feng	Jiu Feng	66, 96
Nurture-Dragon Mountain	Lung Chi	Long Ji	30
Patriarch Sudden-Horse Way-Entire	Ma Tsu	Ma Zu	6, 36
Perpetua-Sands	Ch'ang Sha	Chang Sha	79
Prajna-Devotion	Nan-Yang Hui-Chung	Nan-Yang Hui-Zhong	42
Prosper-Nurture Mountain	Pao Fu	Bao Fu	71
Prosper-Sustain Mountain	Tzu Fu	Zi Fu	25
Purport Dark-Enigma	Lin Chi	Lin Ji	13, 38, 80, 86, 95
Reliance Mountain	Yang Shan	Yang Shan	15, 26, 32, 37, 62, 72, 77, 90
Restore Mountain	Hsiu Shan	Xiu Shan	12, 17, 70
Reward-Perpetua Mountain	Ch'ang Ch'ing	Chang Qing	24, 64, 71
River-Act Mountain	Kuei Shan	Gui Shan	15, 37, 60, 83, 87
Salt-Legal Mountain	Yen Kuan	Yan Guan	25
Shelter-Nation	Hu Kuo	Hu Guo	28
Smuggle Mountain	Chia Shan	Jia Shan	35

ENGLISH	WADE-GILES	PINYIN	SANGHA-CASE
Snow-Chute Mountain	Hsüeh Tou	Xue Dou	26, 34
Snow-Peak Mountain	Hsüeh Feng	Xue Feng	21, 24, 33, 50, 55
Solar-Burgeon Mountain	Hsing Yang	Xing Yang	44
Solar-Strict Mountain	Yen Yang	Yan Yang	57
Solar-Vast Mountain	Ta Yang	Da Yang	89
Source Clearwater	Ch'ing Yüan	Qing Yuan	5
Spirit-Lightning Mountain	Shen Shan	Shen Shan	56
Stealth Mountain	Chia Shan	Jia Shan	68
Stone-Frost Mountain	Shih Shuang	Shi Shuang	68, 89, 96
Three-Sage Mountain	San Sheng	San Sheng	33
Tribute Mountain	Chin Shan	Jin Shan	70
Tumble-Vast Mountain	Ta Sui	Da Sui	30
Twofold Mountain	Tsao Shan	Cao Shan	52, 73
Visitation-Land	Chao Chou	Zhao Zhou	9, 10, 18, 39, 47, 57, 63
Way-I Mountain	Tao Wu	Dao Wu	21, 54, 83
Wellspring-South Mountain	Nan Ch'üan	Nan Quan	9, 10, 16, 23, 67, 69, 79, 91, 93
Wind-Source Mountain	Feng Hsüeh	Feng Xue	29, 33
Wisdom-Hoard	Chih Tsang	Zhi Zang	6
Yellow-Bitterroot Mountain	Huang Po	Huang Bo	53, 86
Yokel-Patriarch Mountain	Lu Tsu	Lu Zu	23, 93

2. Chinese Names with English Equivalents

Wade-Giles	Pinyin	English	Sangha-Case
Chang Ching	Zhang Jing	Manifest-Revere	16
Ch'ang Ch'ing	Chang Qing	Reward-Perpetua Mountain	24, 64, 71
Ch'ang Sha	Chang Sha	Perpetua-Sands	79
Chao Chou	Zhao Zhou	Visitation-Land	9, 10, 18, 39, 47, 57, 63
Chia Shan	Jia Shan	Smuggle Mountain	35
Chia Shan	Jia Shan	Stealth Mountain	68
Ch'ien Feng	Qian Feng	Heaven-Peak Mountain	40, 61
Chih Tsang	Zhi Zang	Wisdom-Hoard	6
Chin Shan	Jin Shan	Tribute Mountain	70
Ch'ing Lin	Qing Lin	Azure-Forest Mountain	59
Ch'ing Yüan	Qing Yuan	Source Clearwater	5
Chiu Feng	Jiu Feng	Nine-Peak Mountain	66, 96
Chu Ti	Zhu Di	Million-Million	84
Chung Yi	Zhong Yi	Bull's-Eye Altar	72
Fa Yen	Fa Yan	Dharma-Eye	17, 20, 27, 51, 64, 74
Feng Hsüeh	Feng Xue	Wind-Source Mountain	29, 33
Hsing Hua	Xing Hua	Burgeon-Change	97
Hsing Yang	Xing Yang	Solar-Burgeon Mountain	44
Hsiu Shan	Xiu Shan	Restore Mountain	12, 17, 70
Hsüan Sha	Xuan Sha	Dark-Enigma-Sands Mountain	21, 24, 81
Hsüeh Feng	Xue Feng	Snow-Peak Mountain	21, 24, 33, 50, 55
Hsüeh Tou	Xue Dou	Snow-Chute Mountain	26, 34
Hu Kuo	Hu Guo	Shelter-Nation	28
Huang Po	Huang Bo	Yellow-Bitterroot Mountain	53, 86
Jui Yen	Rui Yan	Crag-Talisman Mountain	75
Kuei Shan	Gui Shan	River-Act Mountain	15, 37, 60, 83, 87
Lang-ya Chiao	Lang-ya Jiao	Jewel-Fang Awake	100
Lin Chi	Lin Ji	Purport Dark-Enigma	13, 38, 80, 86, 95
Lo P'u	Luo Pu	Far-Waters Mountain	35, 41

Wade-Giles	Pinyin	English	Sangha-Case
Lo Shan	Luo Shan	Gauze Mountain	43
Lu Tsu	Lu Zu	Yokel-Patriarch Mountain	23, 93
Lung Chi	Long Ji	Nurture-Dragon Mountain	30
Lung Ya	Long Ya	Dragon-Fang Mountain	80
Ma Ku	Ma Gu	Flax-Canyon Mountain	16
Ma Tsu	Ma Zu	Patriarch Sudden-Horse Way-Entire	6, 36
Mi Hu	Mi Hu	Mongrol-Grain	62
Nan Ch'üan	Nan Quan	Wellspring-South Mountain	9, 10, 16, 23, 67, 69, 79, 91, 93
Nan-Yang Hui-Chung	Nan-Yang Hui-Zhong	Prajna-Devotion	42
Pao Fu	Bao Fu	Prosper-Nurture Mountain	71
Po (Pai) Chang	Bai Zhang	Hundred-Elder Mountain	6, 8
P'u-T'i Ta-Mo	Pu-Ti Da-Mo	Bodhidharma	2
San Sheng	San Sheng	Three-Sage Mountain	33
Shen Shan	Shen Shan	Spirit-Lightning Mountain	56
Shih Shuang	Shi Shuang	Stone-Frost Mountain	68, 89, 96
Shou Shan	Shou Shan	First Mountain	65, 76
Ta Sui	Da Sui	Tumble-Vast Mountain	30
Ta Yang	Da Yang	Solar-Vast Mountain	89
Tao Wu	Dao Wu	Way-I Mountain	21, 54, 83
Te Shan	De Shan	Mirror-Sight Mountain	55
Te Shan (Hsüan Chien)	De Shan (Xuan Jian)	Heart-Sight Mountain	14, 22, 52
Te Shan (Yüan Ming)	De Shan (Yuan Ming)	Lumen-Whole	46
Ti Tsang	Di Zang	Earth-Hoard Mountain	12, 20, 64
T'ieh Mo	Tie Mo	Iron-Grinder	60
T'ou Tzu	Tou Zi	Dice-Thrown Mountain	63
Tsao Shan	Cao Shan	Twofold Mountain	52, 73
Ts'ui Wei	Cui Wei	Kingfisher Shadowed-Emergence	80
Ts'ui Yen	Cui Yan	Kingfisher-Cliff Mountain	71

WADE-GILES	PINYIN	ENGLISH	SANGHA-CASE
Tung Shan	Dong Shan	Fathom Mountain	22, 49, 56, 80, 89, 94, 98
Tzu Fu	Zi Fu	Prosper-Sustain Mountain	25
Yang Shan	Yang Shan	Reliance Mountain	15, 26, 32, 37, 62, 72, 77, 90
Yao Shan	Yao Shan	Medicine Mountain	7
Yen Kuan	Yan Guan	Salt-Legal Mountain	25
Yen T'ou	Yan Tou	Crag-Summit Mountain	22, 43, 50, 55, 75
Yen Yang	Yan Yang	Solar-Strict Mountain	57
Yün Men	Yun Men	Cloud-Gate Mountain	11, 19, 21, 24, 26, 31, 40, 61, 71, 78, 82, 92, 99
Yün Yen	Yun Yan	Cloud-Crag Mountain	21, 49, 54

Sangha-Cases Included in Other Collections

CAREFREE-EASE RECORD (CA. 1145 C.E.)	BLUE-CLIFF RECORD (CA. 1040)	NO-GATE GATEWAY (1228)
1	92	
2	1	
3		
4		
5		
6	73	
7		
8		2
9	63, 64	14
10		31
11		
12		
13		
14		
15		
16	31	
17		
18		1
19		
20		
21		
22		

CAREFREE-EASE RECORD (CA. 1145 C.E.)	BLUE-CLIFF RECORD (CA. 1040)	NO-GATE GATEWAY (1228)
23		
24	22	
25	91	
26		
27		26
28		
29	38	
30	29	
31	83	
32		
33	49	
34	61	
35		
36	3	
37		
38		
39		7
40		
41		
42		
43		
44		
45		
46		
47		37
48	84	
49		
50	51	
51		
52		
	11	

CAREFREE-EASE RECORD (CA. 1145 C.E.)	BLUE-CLIFF RECORD (CA. 1040)	NO-GATE GATEWAY (1228)
54	89	
55		13
56		
57		
58	97	
59		
60	24	
61		48
62		
63	41	
64		
65		
66		
67		
68		
69		
70		
71	8	
72		
73		
74		
75		
76		
77		
78	77	
79		46
80	20	
81		
82		
83		
84	19	3

CAREFREE-EASE RECORD (CA. 1145 C.E.)	BLUE-CLIFF RECORD (CA. 1040)	NO-GATE GATEWAY (1228)
85	18	
86		
87		
88	94	
89		
90		25
91	40	
92	62	
93		
94		
95		
96		
97		
98		
99	50	
100		